Black Grandparents As Parents

Lenora Madison Poe

2034 Blake Street
Berkeley, California 94704

ISBN 0-9633992-0-9
LIBRARY OF CONGRESS
516-580

Black Grandparents As Parents

To my grandchildren, Moriah Faith Burke and Lynn Michaelle Poe

Contents

Acknowledgments

This book is dedicated to the memory of my beloved parents, the late Tommie and Carrie Madison, who always gave me love, support, and encouragement. In raising fifteen children, they provided a model of parenting that remains a permanent source of inspiration to me.

My very special thanks also go to the grandparents who participated in this study, without whose help this book could not exist.

I am grateful to Drs. Anna Hazan, Debra Johnson, Floyd Wylie, and Anselm Strauss for the help, patience, understanding, and encouragement they showed during the course of this study.

I deeply appreciate the support of Assemblyman Tom Bates of the 12th Assembly District of California, who has made many legislative efforts to assist grandparents who are raising their grandchildren.

I would also like to collectively thank several members of the Department of Social Services in Alameda County and many staff members of Children's Hospital Medical Center in Oakland, who offered valuable information.

Many thanks to Bananas, Inc., of Oakland, for providing a meeting place and logistical assistance at no cost to my Grandparents As Parents support group.

I am also immensely grateful to Dr. Paul Weisser for his skillful and painstaking editing of my manuscript.

Finally, I sincerely thank my husband, Levi, for his patience, love, and understanding throughout this research, and my children, Michael, Angela, Terry, and Michaelle, for their constant encouragement.

Introduction

This is a study of the emotional adjustment of grandparents who are providing primary parenting responsibilities for their grandchildren. Currently, there are no recorded studies that explore the roles, responsibilities, and problems of grandparents who are performing the primary parenting function for their grandchildren. Yet, there is a growing consensus among social-service professionals that never before in recent history have so many grandparents served as surrogate parents to their grandchildren. Few studies have examined how this arrangement of grandparents parenting their grandchildren affects the various members of the family. This is an increasingly important area of study because of the large number of children, especially minority children, who are now being parented by their grandparents.

Many of the biological parents of these grandchildren are substance abusers in an era of epidemic drug use. Thus, many of these grandchildren are born to drug-addicted parents or to parents who are or have been incarcerated. Many of these grandchildren's parents are single teenagers or parents who are divorced or deceased.

Black Grandparents As Parents

Grandparents take on the parenting responsibilities of their grand-children as an alternative to foster placement with nonrelatives. These grandparents, in many instances, are the only persons standing between their grandchildren and foster placement. They are willing, at an age when they could normally expect to be "phasing out" caretaking roles, to start parenting all over again by raising their grandchildren.

Significance of the Problem

It is virtually impossible to estimate, at this point, the number of grandparents who are currently providing primary, though often unof-ficial, care for their grandchildren. We do know that nearly 2.3 million children live in their grandparents' homes (Accinelli, 1988). Local social-service officials in Alameda and Contra Costa Counties in Northern California estimate that more than 1,000 grandparents in these counties are caring for grandchildren who have been left unprotected by their "crack"-addicted parents. The *East Bay Express* ("Grandmothers on the Line," 1989) reported that many of these grandparents are single women who are on fixed incomes and are themselves divorced or widowed. Accompanying the increased addiction to "crack" cocaine by young parents, and the accelerating breakdown of the family, are the additional problems of a lack of positive role models and the absence of economic opportunities for youth.

Family historians (Johnson, 1983; Bongaarts, Menken, & Watkins, 1984; Cherlin & Furstenberg, 1986) all agree that as grandparents take on the primary parenting responsibilities of their grandchildren, they are being deprived of a wholesome and more typical grandparent-grand-

2

Introduction

child relationship. Developmentally, their lives are often disrupted, affecting retirement, leisure time activities, and social interactions. Grandparents who are parenting their grandchildren may experience major disruptions in their families that may create very dysfunctional situations for them as well as their grandchildren.

Despite the widespread recognition of the increasing number of children being raised by their grandparents, there are currently no official statistics or estimates of the number of families consisting of grandparents and grandchildren. Martin O'Connell (1988), Chief of the Fertility Statistics Branch of the U.S. Census Bureau, reported that, as of March 1986, the nation had 63 million households. He estimated that approximately 1.7 million of these households consisted of people 55 years or older who were living with their grandchildren, probably as their primary caretakers.

The present study sought to gain a greater understanding of the psychological impact of assuming primary care of one's grandchildren. Fourteen grandparents who, in total, had been parenting thirty grandchildren for a minimum of two years were interviewed concerning the impact of such an arrangement on their own lives, the lives of their children, and the lives of their grandchildren. Of particular interest to this study was how the resumption of the parenting role was affecting these grandparents developmentally. As will be seen in the discussion of the findings, at a time when they expected to lay down the burdens of jobs and child rearing, these grandparents are making great personal sacrifices to care for their neglected or abandoned grandchildren.

It is hoped that the findings of the present study will describe more fully the needs and experiences of the grandparents, parents, and children in such disrupted families. It is also hoped that the findings can be used by planners of social policy to better address the legal, social, and psychological needs of all the family members.

Traditional Roles of Grandparents

It is assumed that, for most people with adult children, becoming a grandparent is a pleasant occasion. Most grandparents are only marginally involved in the rearing of their grandchildren. In most families, according to Cherlin and Furstenberg (1986), "grandparents serve as a latent source of support for their grandchildren, ready to step in when needed" (p. 133). Many grandparents whose children are addicted to drugs, however, are denied the traditional rewards associated with being grandparents. Instead, they are being forced to begin parenting all over again because their own adult children are either unwilling or unable to care for themselves, much less parent their children. The "crack" epidemic has exacerbated the problem, leaving an increasing number of grandparents to face the legal, financial, emotional, and physical burden of child rearing.

Some sociologists and family historians (Johnson, 1983; Cherlin & Furstenberg, 1986; Franklin, 1989) have reported that, under the best of circumstances, new grandparental roles involve new conflicts. The major conflict, according to these authors, involves the grandparents' desire for independence and personal satisfaction as opposed to their feelings of family obligations and their desire to have good relationships with their grandchildren.

Under ordinary circumstances, when a person becomes a grandparent, there are usually few family roles competing for his or her time and

Introduction

attention. Grandparenthood is normally a separate stage of family life, unfettered by child-care obligations. However, Bongaarts, Menken, and Watkins (1984) reported that grandparents who must provide primary parenting for their grandchildren assume long-term parental obligations.

In a study of the roles and functions of grandparents during their child's divorce, Johnson (1985) found that grandparents tend to serve as auxiliary support for their grandchildren during the divorce of their parents. The grandparents do not, as a rule, provide the primary parenting for these grandchildren. Johnson organized this research around the five following categories that the grandparents used in defining their role with their grandchildren: (1) contrasts between the traditional images of the grandparents and contemporary redefinitions; (2) the use of age norms in their definitions of the role; (3) role models in the grandparents' family; (4) situation determinants stemming from the divorce; and (5) comparisons between grandparent-grandchild relationships before the divorce and after the divorce of the biological parents.

Johnson's study consisted of white middle-class families who lived in Marin County, California, and therefore may be limited in its generalizability to other families in other locations or ethnic backgrounds. Johnson elucidates the nature of the problem of the erosion of the family structure, stating that with the family system undergoing major changes through frequent divorce, remarriage, and the drug epidemic, family researchers have been slow to recognize that grandparents are increasingly necessary as a stabilizing force in the American family. Apple (1956) and Schneider (1968) found that there is a wide structural separation between generations in the American family system, which results in autonomy and privacy in the nuclear family and, subsequently, a remote status for the grandparents. However, as Johnson's study and the present study indicate, grandparents cease to be remote and rather become quite central when there is a disruption in the parental generation.

Reasons Grandparents Are Parenting Their Grandchildren

Families consisting of grandparents who are primary caretakers of their grandchildren are a rapidly growing social phenomenon in this country. As stated previously, there are several reasons why this is occurring, particularly among minority families. Many biological parents of these grandchildren have grown up in an era of epidemic drug use. Thus, many grandchildren are born to drug-addicted parents or to parents who are divorced and are not equipped to care for their children. Grandparents are often called on to become primary caretakers for these grandchildren as an alternative to foster placement with nonrelatives. According to DeToledo (1988), the most common reasons for children being placed with their grandparents are: parental neglect or abandonment of the children; parental physical and/or sexual abuse of the children; death of the parents by illness, accident, or suicide; parental involvement with drugs and/or alcohol; incarceration of the parents; and mental illness of the parents.

It is commonly believed that, during the Great Depression, large numbers of parents, both black and white, were unable to care for their children. There is documentation for the number of white children who

Introduction

were placed in orphanages; however, there are no recorded figures for black or white children who were raised by their grandparents. Today, both black and white grandparents are raising their grandchildren because society assumes that children separated from their parents should be placed with other relatives whenever possible. LaMotte (1988) indicated that the focus of the Department of Children's Services has always been on placing children in the homes of relatives. She reported that California state law requires that a relative be the first choice of placement for children if the parents are unable to care for them. Colon (1978) argued that when children are placed with their relatives, they report feeling closer to their family than if they are placed in foster care with nonrelatives. Colon expressed a strong need for the placed child to maintain access to his or her biological "rootedness." What has been missing to date is research on the effects of these arrangements on the grandparents.

According to Staples (1971), estimates of the number of grandchildren living with grandparents are difficult to obtain because the arrangements of placing grandchildren with their grandparents are normally made hastily in times of crisis and, initially, for only a few months, although many of these "temporary" arrangements extend into years. Some children have been placed with their grandparents through the juvenile court system, against the wishes of the parents. This arrangement can create an additional difficulty for the grandparents because the relationship between them and their children becomes strained, along with their having to manage new parenting responsibilities with their grandchildren. This conflict often results in the grandchildren feeling like pawns.

Black Grandparents As Parents

Factors Affecting the Family's Adjustment

In my psychotherapy practice, I have found that the specific reason that children have to be placed in the care of their grandparents can make a difference in everyone's adjustment to the situation. For example, in the simplest, albeit most dramatic, case—the death of a parent through accident or illness—the grandparents often adopt their grandchildren. These grandparents have no fear that the children will be taken away from them, nor do they fear that someone will interfere with their parenting roles. The grandparents tend not to blame their own children for the disruption of their lives. The immediate problems involve the grandparents mourning the loss of their children and the grandchildren mourning the loss of their parents. This mourning can eventually end, because everyone knows the placement is final and lifelong. In my experience, the number of grandparents caring for their grandchildren in these circumstances represents a small portion of those grandparents who are providing primary care for their grandchildren. In circumstances such as the parents' death or illness, grandparents tend to get more support from their family, friends, and state agencies than if the reason for assuming such care is inadequate parenting by their adult children.

As will be shown in this study's findings, the adjustment that other family members (other children and relatives) make to the grandparents providing primary care for their grandchildren depends on a variety of factors: for example, the legal status of the children; the situation that led to the children being placed with the grandparents; whether or not the biological parents reside in the grandparents' home; and the age, health, and other resources of the grandparents.

Introduction

Some grandparents who are providing primary care for their grandchildren have their own children residing in the home. When the parents of the grandchildren are living, the grandparents may have either informal or formal custody of these grandchildren. With informal custody (in which no state agency is involved), the grandparents usually receive no financial support for the grandchildren. This situation often begins as a temporary arrangement for the grandparents, with the grandchildren being placed with them in a time of crisis (Stone, 1989).

Whether court-ordered custody is of a formal or informal nature, there is still an impact on the family's adjustment. In each case, the child is a dependent of the court. However, with formal placement of grandchildren with their grandparents, the latter are legal guardians and can obtain welfare and medical insurance benefits for their grandchildren. By contrast, with informal custody, the court retains guardianship, and thus the grandparents may not be eligible for similar kinds of social-service assistance. This can be very difficult for the grandparents, since they do not have the authority to make decisions regarding their grandchildren. The biological parents or the courts may have decision-making authority over the children.

Despite the growing prevalence of arrangements (formal or informal) in which grandparents are providing primary care for their grandchildren, and despite the number of lives involved in these arrangements, past research has tended to focus on the emotional effects on the children. For example, Mauluccio and Sinonoglu (1981) recommended that children in placement with their grandparents should maintain some relationship with their biological parents even after being separated from them. If such a relationship is not maintained, the authors argued, love may mingle with anger and disappointment—although these feelings are usually hidden or denied by the children, who may lack an appropriate outlet to express them. Such angry and disappointed feelings may have a profound and negative effect upon a child's personality.

However, as will be seen in the discussion of the findings of the present study, the health and age of the grandparents providing primary care for their grandchildren will also affect everyone's adaptation to this new family arrangement. For example, many younger grandparents still have jobs; they want to be with family and friends and have fun; and they tend to be active and have competing commitments. Older grandparents, on the other hand, tend to have been looking forward to retirement and leisure; they tend to have feweroutside commitments; and they tend to be significantly less family-oriented in their social network and lifestyle. Lawson (1988) reported that "at an age when these grandparents least expect it, when they have other plans on how to spend their 'sunset' years, an increasing number of grandparents are finding themselves again raising younger children" (p. 8). These grandparents usually do not have the patience, the energy, the stamina, or the financial resources that they had when they were younger and parenting their own children. The most important source of variation in grandparenting behavior and psychological well-being, as noted by Johnson (1985), appears to be the age of the grandparents and the grandchildren.

Difficulties Associated with Prenatal "Crack" Exposure

Approximately 40 percent of the grandchildren in this study were identified as born "crack"-exposed (see Appendix A). In most cases,

10

these children, ranging in age from infancy through 8 years, are likely to have suffered prenatal "crack" exposure along with poor prenatal care. According to the grandparents, taking care of these grandchildren requires much time and energy. To begin with, the children often need constant and vigilant medical attention that can cause the grandparents many sleepless nights.

According to Lewis, Bennett, and Schmeder (1989), babies born "crack"-exposed exhibit signs of fine motor tremors of the hands, arms, and legs; they have unusual responses to stimuli in their environment; they typically exhibit sucking and swallowing difficulties; they experience disturbances in their sleep and wake cycle; and they are usually quite irritable and show visual and auditory inattentiveness.

For most grandparents who parent prenatal "crack"-exposed children, their most ardent task has been trying to help the children recover from their traumatic experiences—for example, abuse, abandonment, and neglect. Lewis, Bennett, and Schmeder (1989) noted that "prenatal cocaine-exposed infants experience a significant number of startle and tremor responses. They may experience a disruption in their orientation and motor response" (p. 326). In contrast, according to these authors, "a normal infant shuts out intrusive stimuli, takes in positive stimuli, and modulates movements" (p. 667). Farrar and Kearns (1989) stated that "infants exposed to cocaine *in utero* appear to have significant depression of organizational response to environmental stimuli" (p. 667). According to these experts, these infants were found to be small for gestational age, compared with infants with no prenatal cocaine exposure. These authors also agree that prenatal cocaine-exposed infants may experience cerebral infarction and associated seizure activity.

Summary of the Problem

The present study focused primarily on the grandparents' views of their roles and responsibilities as they parent their grandchildren. This study explored what changes and adjustments grandparents experienced in their lives as they took on the parenting role for their grandchildren. Also examined were ways that this role affected everyone in the family and how parenting their grandchildren may have affected the grandparents' relationship with their own adult children.

Data on grandparents parenting their grandchildren were collected from participants through unstructured interviews, as well as the researcher's regular participation as a volunteer professional facilitator at ongoing monthly Grandparents As Parents (GAP) meetings.

An early problem that surfaced in the present research is the paucity of previous studies that focus on grandparents who are providing primary care for their grandchildren. The importance of recognizing and identifying the structure and the characteristics of the entire support system for grandparents as parents has been grossly unrecognized by society in general. Thus, this is clearly a fertile field for discovery.

1

Review of the Literature

An Overview

Few studies have examined the psychological effects on grandparents who serve as surrogate parents to their grandchildren. Recent studies in this area have not examined the emotional impact on and the emotional adjustments of grandparents as they assume the primary parenting role of their grandchildren. Despite the growing prevalence of arrangements (formal or informal) in which grandparents are providing primary care for their grandchildren, and despite the number of lives involved in these arrangements, past research has focused primarily on the emotional effects on the children.

Clinical experience, sociological theory, and psychotherapy case studies (McAdoo, 1985; Johnson, 1985; DeToledo, 1988; Franklin, 1989) all indicate that as family relationships are influenced by emotional and physical upheavals, grandparents are increasingly necessary as a stabilizing force in the American family.

Glick (cited in McAdoo, 1985) noted that, prior to the past decade, if a mother left her children, she did so while moving elsewhere to earn

13

a living. There is a current increase in the numbers of grandparents parenting their grandchildren because the biological parents are either unable or unwilling to do so, primarily because of their drug involvement.

Jones (1973) reported that the nature of the grandmother's role appears to be a function of culture, family dependency, and sociohistorical tradition. However, according to Apple (1956) and Schneider (1968), there is a wide structural separation between generations in the American family system, which results in autonomy and privacy in the nuclear family. This has led to a remote status for the grandparents.

Atchley, Miller, and Troll (1979) noted that "because of early marriages and early childbirths, grandparenthood is more recently being considered a middle-aged phenomenon rather than one of old age" (p. 108). These authors found that a growing number of grandparents are in their mid-forties, whereas grandparenthood traditionally began in the fifties and sixties. Sprey and Matthews (1981) noted that demographic evidence shows that contemporary grandparenthood often begins in early middle age; the median age at the birth of the first grandchild is now 45 years.

Many black grandparents have continued to raise their younger children after their older children have left home and married. Under these conditions, being grandparents often overlaps with being a parent (Bongaarts, Menken, & Watkins, 1984).

Johnson (1983) examined how the grandmother's chronological age affects her relationship with her grandchildren. She found that the older grandmothers are significantly less family-oriented than the younger ones, while the younger grandmothers are more approving of traveling and enjoying social outlets. This evidence suggests, Johnson noted, that chronological age determines the frequency of contact with grandchildren. Older grandmothers have significantly less contact with their grandchildren. It is important to note that Johnson's study examined the grandparents' role with their grandchildren when the biological parents of these grandchildren were divorced. These grandparents served essentially as auxiliary support to their grandchildren, unlike the grandparents in the present study, who are providing primary parenting for their grandchildren. However, it will be interesting to see if age is a factor in the adjustment of the grandparents in this study.

Cherlin and Furstenberg (1986) reported that "changes in families in the United States have been a long-term process in which cultural changes have influenced the evolution of the grandparents/grandchild relationship" (p. 46). Because significant societal changes have occurred in today's family structure, grandparents are becoming the primary cohesive and stabilizing forces in their grandchildren's lives. They are performing the primary parenting role of their grandchildren because of the drug problems of the biological parents of these children. These children are experiencing a "cutoff" from their biological parents.

Colon (1978) believed that children who experience "cutoff" from their biological "rootedness" may be prone to duplicate destructive family patterns in their interpersonal and family relationships. Colon indicated that children's contact with their biological parents is considered a basic ingredient in the children's process of achieving integration in their lives.

Most studies on the welfare of children agree that the children's loyalty to their biological parents is a primary concern. Nagy and Spark (1973), for example, emphasized that children maintain their obligations to their biological family, and children who feel rejected by their

15

biological parents will carry a sense of disloyalty that will have a bearing on their behavior.

Current Studies and Theoretical Models

As has been previously stated, some researchers have looked at the function of grandparents in divorced families. Johnson (1985), for example, studied the role of the grandmother with her grandchildren when the parents of these children were divorced. Johnson found that with the family system undergoing major changes (particularly, frequent divorce and remarriage), family researchers have been slow to recognize that grandparents are increasingly necessary as a stabilizing force in the American family. Johnson further noted that after the divorce of their adult children, the grandparents' nebulous relationship with their grandchildren becomes distant. She attributed this to the strained relationship the grandparents may have with their adult children. Throughout her study, Johnson identified significant factors that influence the grandparents' actions, such as their objective social characteristics, their age, their kinship relationships (maternal or paternal), and their competing commitments stemming from work, marriage, and social affiliations.

Most researchers on grandparenthood agree that the manner in which the grandparents' role is performed is likely to be based on personal qualities and individual options (Furstenberg, 1980; Johnson, 1985; Cherlin & Furstenberg, 1986). Such studies imply that the grandparents' role is an achieved rather than an ascribed one.

Johnson (1983), researching the meaning of grandparenthood, noted that "traditionally grandparents will reject any authority function with their grandchildren in order to retain a friendly and fun-loving image" (p. 90). This avoidance of a disciplinary role with their grandchildren supports the grandparents' attempt to satisfy the grandchildren's needs for pleasure as well as the needs of the grandparents to have a positive grandparent-grandchildren relationship.

The role of the grandmother is one of the most central ones in black families. Franklin (1989) noted that in many black families, the grandmother remains a major power even if the mother is present as the primary caretaker of the children. Because of the current drug epidemic that is striking families across the country, there is an increase in the number of children who are placed in the primary care of their grandparents. According to McAdoo (1985), while a declining proportion of children have been living with a widowed parent, an increasing proportion of children have been living apart from either parent. The great majority of these children, McAdoo found, live with grandparents or other relatives.

As reported by McAdoo (1985), the most recent information on black children under age 18 living with their grandparents was obtained in 1970. That data showed that children living with grandparents constituted about 5 percent of all black children. That was about three times the percentage (1.5%) of children of other races living with their grandparents. Glick (1985) found that another 5 percent of these children lived with one or both parents in the home of the children's grandparents. In these circumstances, Glick noted, many of the mothers may have left their children in the care of the grandparents while they themselves searched for better education or attempted to become more employable.

Franklin (1989) emphasizes the importance of the prestige and dignity of the black grandmother, who, during and after slavery, has traditionally been considered the "guardian of the generation," and who has not ceased to watch over the destiny of black families. Franklin further notes that "the role of the grandmother is considered one of the most central ones in black families. It can also be considered one of the most complex and problematic roles" (p. 71).

Recent research has shown that, traditionally, grandparents have only been marginally involved in the rearing of their grandchildren. In most families, grandparents serve as a latent source of support, ready to step in when needed (Johnson, 1985; Cherlin & Furstenberg, 1986; Franklin, 1989). According to Johnson (1985), the majority of grandparents today are not ordinarily compelled to respond to the parenting needs of their grandchildren. When grandparents are free to assume the traditional grandparent role with their grandchildren, this allows both the grandparent and grandchild to enjoy a more relaxed relationship. Benedek (1959), for example, noted that grandparents often enjoy their grandchildren more than they enjoyed their own children.

It is important to ask what kind of experience grandparents have when they take up the role of primary caretaker for their grandchildren. Do they feel deprived of the relaxed and corrective relationships that Johnson and Benedek have described?

Issues of Adult Development

Researchers in the field of adult development (Neugarten, 1968; Miller, 1976; Levinson, 1978) all agree that as grandparents take on the primary parenting responsibilities of their grandchildren, they are being deprived of their own developmental age- and stage-appropriate activi-

Review of the Literature

ties. Levinson noted that individual personalities may change during the adult years, but these changes are produced by external influences rather than by a developmental sequence. Levinson identified patterned stages in one's life, which include courtship, marriage without children, family with children at home, empty nest, grandparenthood, and beyond. During the grandparenthood stage, Levinson noted, adults experience developmental unfolding from which they may enjoy their anticipated leisure social options as well as the role of being grandparents to their grandchildren.

As stated above, when grandparents take on the responsibilities of parenting their grandchildren, they are deprived of many age- and stage-appropriate activities. Grau and Susser (1989) reported that aging automatically brings some rewards to women in many cultures. Some of these rewards may be identified as: (a) retirement after working for many years; (b) an absence from parenting once their own children have become grown and moved away from home; (c) the enjoyment of leisure time; (d) the availability of traveling; and (e) pursuing some of their personal goals that may have been put on hold while parenting their own children.

Kalish (as cited in Henig, 1988) asserts that:

> Something is assumed to be wrong with older people who wish to sit around and talk with their elderly friends, who wish to stay home and read, who thoroughly enjoy television, and who, for whatever reason, prefer their world to be comfortable, comforting, and manageable, rather than stimulating, challenging, and risky. (p. 254)

Grau and Susser (1989) found that elderly persons traditionally seek to prevent their social isolation. They tend to select friends who are similar to them in such characteristics as age, life status, gender, and socioeconomic status. Jackson (1980) found that many aged persons who are no longer working and are free from child-rearing responsibilities have an increased amount of leisure time. "Most of these elders," she wrote, "spent much of their leisure time socializing with friends, watching television, sleeping, going for walks, and just doing nothing or sitting and thinking" (p. 151). In addition, she noted, many aged persons frequently focus their leisure time by participating in formal social activities—for example, political or community organizations, church activities, sororities, and fraternities.

Jung (1971) maintained that adult development is a process of "midlife individuation," which begins at about age 40 and may continue throughout the remaining years. Jung identified age 40 as the beginning of the "noon of life" in adult development (p. 268). Neugarten (1968) noted that if psychologists are to discover order in the events of adulthood, and if they are to discover order in the changes that occur in all individuals as they age, the social as well as the biological issues should be addressed. Neugarten argued that social definitions of age and age-appropriate behaviors should be more integrated into the study of the adult life cycle. Levinson (1978) also believed that the influence of external social and cultural factors on the "phasing" and progress of the life course should be considered a major aspect of the adult developmental life cycle.

As grandparents parent their grandchildren, they experience significant social and emotional developmental intrusions in their lives. It seems reasonable to assume that they are being deprived of major developmental options that they anticipated during their earlier years. The present study will examine how grandparents assuming such parenting responsibilities adjust to and experience these changes.

2

Methods

Participants

The participants for this study were fourteen black grandparents between the ages of 45 and 70 who reside in the San Francisco Bay Area. I interviewed thirteen grandmothers and one grandfather. All the interviewees had custody of at least one grandchild for a minimum of two years. In every case, these grandparents obtained custody of their grandchild(ren), either formally or informally, because at least one of the biological parents of the child(ren) was addicted to "crack" and was therefore unable to function as a parent.

I recruited the participants in this study from a Grandparents As Parents (GAP) support group that is sponsored by Bananas, Inc., a child-care referral agency in Oakland in which I participate as a professional facilitator.

The GAP support group had its first meeting in November 1988. It has continued to meet on a regular basis since January 1989. Although new people periodically join the group, most of the members have been in it since its inception. The meetings are held on the first and third Mondays of each month from 7:30 to 9:00 P.M.

The average attendance at the meetings has been approximately fifteen grandparents, usually grandmothers. The group is approximately 95 percent black and 98 percent female. The format is basically unstructured, providing a forum for the grandparents to freely discuss their issues and concerns related to parenting their grandchildren.

Procedure

I invited fourteen of these grandparents to participate in this study by being interviewed for anywhere from an hour and a half to two and a half hours, to answer questions that focused on their experiences and responsibilities in relation to their parental role with their grandchildren. The individual interviews began approximately four months after the first GAP support group meeting. The interviews were held in the grandparents' homes. I conducted two interviews per month, so interviewing fourteen grandparents took me seven months to complete. The GAP group membership changed, but the interviewing remained separate from the group. All interviewees remained with the group throughout the data collection stage. However, three grandparents who returned their grandchildren to the parents left the group shortly thereafter.

I audiotaped the interviews, had the tapes transcribed, and then I coded them line by line. I prepared case summaries to create a preliminary exploratory study and to generate preliminary categories for analysis. I constantly compared information from the interviews and the GAP support group meetings to refine concepts of the study. The findings for this study were based on my analysis of the data.

Methods

Because of the complex history of my involvement with the GAP group, I used multiple methods of research. Fieldwork was the primary method. The specific field methods I used were participant-observation, clinical interviews, and social action. Using these methods, I gained access to the world of these grandparents. I explored their experiences through my roles as facilitator, participant-observer, and clinical interviewer. As I will describe later, social action was an unanticipated product of these efforts and served as affirmation of the social value of the project.

Fieldwork. McCall and Simmons (1969) reported that the essential issue in any field research is the assumption by the researcher of some position in a structure of relationships. In the present case, I acted as facilitator and counselor for the GAP support group. Schatzman and Strauss (1973) argued that field research should not be taken as the functional equivalent of laboratory research. Thus, what transpired between me (as the researcher) and the grandparents (as representatives of the population being studied) was inductive and emergent rather than deductive.

The field method process of discovery, Schatzman and Strauss noted, may lead the researcher to the basic analytic theme after moving through much of the substance in the field. However, problem statements in field research may emerge at any point in the research process, even toward the very end. Hence, I postulated no preliminary hypotheses for this study, and concepts began to emerge almost immediately. Schatzman and Strauss further noted that field researchers should concern themselves less with whether their techniques are "scientific" than with what specific operations might yield the most meaningful information.

Participant-Observation. McCall and Simmons (1969) defined the role of the participant-observer and the images that respondents hold of him or her as central to the definitions of the participant-observer's position. The circumstances under which the participant-observer works and the type of data collected are shaped by these factors. I was sensitive to the dangers of the grandparents incorporating and idealizing their perceptions of my values and my position within the group. McCall and Simmons argued that the participant-observer is faced with two types of problems as he or she sets out to collect data: (1) the tactical problem of maneuver in the field; and (2) the evaluation of data.

Gaining entree in the field is often difficult, as Schatzman and Strauss (1973) noted, but for me this was not the case. One of the tactical problems I experienced with this research was the rapidity with which the grandparents took me in. In the initial stages, the grandparents tried very hard to please me and to meet what they perceived to be my expectations.

The success of my developing relationship with the group was a great aid to me as I became involved. However, some serious fieldwork problems grew out of this relationship as I became keenly aware of the possibility of becoming overly identified with the grandparents. As the group continued to meet bimonthly, many of the grandparents invested confidence and hope that the group would make a difference for them. They were clearly beginning to idealize me, referring to me as their "savior" and expressing the hope that I could rescue them from their social and family isolation. The issue of personal bias is one danger in

Methods

such situations. I felt at this point that I was required to deal with the issue of clarifying and defining my role as clinician and scholar in order to manage an untenable emerging dependent relationship with some of the grandparents in the group. I attempted to handle these role conflicts by remaining objective yet supportive.

Because I was aware of my personal biases, which may have been revealed through facial expressions and body language, I attempted to prevent any observable distortions of my response to any information shared by the respondents. However, the data collected by participant-observers, except as they report personal experiences, cannot be independent of their study sample's ability and willingness to report (McCall & Simmons, 1969). Hence, the quality of my relationship with the grandparents in this study was central. I dealt with this by preserving clinical distance while encouraging the grandparents to talk openly and freely about their individual experiences of parenting their grandchildren.

McCall and Simmons (1969) noted that field-workers can overly identify with informants and start to lose their research perspective by "going native." I realized that I had become too identified with these grandparents and had to maintain an acceptable margin that would not interfere with the quality of my research. However, these field research problems were not damaging to the research per se, because the data were primarily drawn from the clinical one-on-one interviews.

Clinical Interviews. The theoretical basis of my use of the clinical-interview method derived largely from case-study techniques that are prevalent in psychotherapy, and also from participant-observation methods used in disciplines such as sociology and anthropology

(Blumenfeld, 1983). From a psychological perspective, Sullivan (1970) noted that the principal instrument in an interview is the interviewer's personality. The processes that constitute the data that can be subjected to scientific study occur, Sullivan argued, not in the study sample, nor in the observer, but in the situation that is created *between* the researcher and the respondents. Freud (1963) stated that interviewees should be encouraged to relate everything that passes through their minds, even if they think it is unimportant or irrelevant. Freud placed special emphasis on the interviewees not omitting any thought or idea from their experience because it may be embarrassing or painful to them. Some grandparents in the present study felt uncomfortable acknowledging their experience of parenting their grandchildren because this was a painful admission to them. Others felt embarrassed admitting that their own children had chosen drug addiction and/or involvement. As my relationship with them matured, these fears began to dissipate.

Glaser and Strauss (1967) defined the clinical method of interviewing as a naturalistic interview technique that includes participant-observations and other field methods that emphasize the observer as the primary recording instrument. In this respect, the quality of the interaction between researcher and respondent is not unlike the case-study technique prevalent in clinically oriented disciplines.

Social Action. Although this may not be an orthodox field method, social action quickly became part of my experience, and I felt the importance of reporting it. Glaser (1978) noted that society focuses on social-psychological issues through highlighting, becoming, or personalizing experiences. Through the GAP support group, the experiences of grandparents parenting their grandchildren were highlighted not only

Methods

in various news media programs (newspapers, local and national television, and radio talk shows) but also in local social-action programs such as Grandparents Celebration in the city of Oakland and local legislative hearings in San Francisco and Sacramento. This was a part of the process from the inception of the GAP support group.

Bananas invited Deanne Stone, a news reporter, to attend the first GAP support group meeting, which was held on November 14, 1988. This was the beginning of media exposure for the group. However, within five months (May 1989) after the original group began meeting on a regular monthly basis, I was called by Carolyn Newberg, of the *Oakland Tribune*, and asked to be interviewed for an article on "Children in Crisis." On September 25, 1989, Dianne Brooks, of *The Sunday Argus* (Hayward, California), asked for and was granted permission to observe the GAP support group, and subsequently wrote an article entitled "These Children Deserve Life." On November 17, 1989, Craig Anderson, of the *East Bay Express* (Berkeley, California), was granted permission to observe the GAP group, and he wrote an article entitled "Grandmothers on the Line."

In May 1989, five grandparents from the GAP support group appeared on a local television program, "48-Hour Crack Street." In October 1989, three grandparents appeared with me at a legislative hearing in San Francisco before Assemblyman Tom Bates. The subject, "The Changing Family," included the role and needs of grandparents who are parenting their grandchildren. In April 1990, two grandparents and I were invited to attend a state legislative hearing in Sacramento before Assemblyman Bates, to testify on Assembly Bill No. 1060, addressing the financial needs of grandparents who parent their grandchildren. In May 1990, four grandparents appeared on local television, on KPIX's "The Evolution of Motherhood." On June 18, 1990, a number of grandparents from the GAP support group appeared on national television on NBC's "Today Show."

The media became interested in the issue of grandparents who parent their grandchildren because of the prevalence of the drug epidemic in this country. The grandparents were themselves beginning to search for assistance and support because of the increasing demands on them. Political and social awareness of these issues began to surface because of the social action of these grandparents.

Instruments

Within the first few sessions of the GAP support group, I developed a series of fifteen research guides that formed the basis for both the clinical interview and the open-ended discussions within the group meetings themselves (see Table 1). In addition, prior to beginning each interview, I asked each participant a series of demographic questions (see Table 2).

Methods

Table 1

General Interview Guidelines

1. Circumstances that led to the child(ren) being placed with the grandparent.

    a. What were the circumstances that made it necessary for you to take responsibility for parenting your grandchild(ren)?

    b. When did you become aware that the placement of your grandchild(ren) in your home was not a temporary placement? (Probe for reaction to each stage.)

2. Impact of placement on grandparent's life.

    a. How has parenting your grandchild(ren) affected your life? (Probe for [1] changes in health; [2] sense of independence; [3] future goals; [4] social life; [5] leisure time; [6] peer relationship; and [7] relationship with own children.)

    b. Describe the major changes you have had to make as you took on the responsibility of parenting your grandchild(ren).

    c. Would you say you have to make sacrifices to care for your grandchild(ren)? What are they?

    d. Are there specific benefits you have gained by having your grandchild(ren) with you?

    e. In all, how do you feel about becoming the primary caretaker of your grandchild(ren)? What do you like best? What do you like least?

3. Relationship between grandparent and their own child(ren).

    a. What was your relationship with your daughter (or son) like before you took over the parenting of your grandchild(ren)?

    b. What has your relationship with your daughter (or son) been like since you took over the parenting of your grandchild(ren)?

    c. In what ways is your relationship with your daughter (or son) closer (more distant) now?

    d. Does your daughter (or son) share parenting responsibilities?

    e. How does she/he support your parenting of their child(ren)?

    f. What are the areas of conflict?

4. Identification of needs that society could better serve.

    a. What individual, groups, or resources have been most helpful to you as you have assumed primary care for your grandchild(ren)? How have they been useful?

    b. Are there ways that specific individuals, groups, or resources could be more helpful?

Black Grandparents As Parents

Table 2
Demographics   **ID No.** _____

Grandparent Marital Status
    Married _____
    Divorced _____
    Widowed _____
    Single _____
    Living with partner _____
No. years of education _____
Number of other adults living in household _____
Work Status
    Full-time employed _____
    Part-time employed _____
    Retired _____
    Disability _____
    Unemployed _____
Occupation _____
Living Arrangement
    House _____   own/rent _____
    Apartment _____
    Condo _____
    Other _____
Number of grandchildren you are parenting? _____ M _____ F _____
Grandchildren you are parenting   Age ___   Gender ___
                                           ___   ___
                                           ___   ___
                                           ___   ___
                                           ___   ___
                                           ___   ___
Are you parenting your daughter's child(ren)?   Yes ___ No ___
Are you parenting your son's child(ren)?   Yes ___ No ___
The age of your grandchild(ren)'s mother (your daughter) _____
    or
The age of your grandchild(ren)'s father (your son) _____
Does your grandchild(ren)'s parent (your son or daughter) live with you in your
    home?   Yes ___ No ___
Did anyone else take care of your children when they were small?
    Yes ___   No ___
How many times have you been married? _____

Methods

It should be noted that I used the interview questions only as a guide. Both in the interviews and in the group discussions, I encouraged the grandparents to speak freely, to cover the issues most pressing to them. The data for this study thus comprised all the material I elicited from the grandparents concerning their experiences as primary caretakers of their grandchildren. The data came from the interviews, the group discussions, and the grandparents' own testimony to reporters and legislators.

I took process notes and wrote memos about each GAP group discussion. I also noted my observations after listening to the grandparents interact with members of the media or the legislature, paying particular attention to the issues the grandparents identified as important to them. These notes and memos became my participant-observation and interview data, which were the major source for the results that follow.

Analysis of the Data

Qualitative Method. For this study, I used the qualitative approach as a theoretical base and the grounded theory method of data analysis. The clinical approach and grounded theory have in common that they deal with experimental data. Hancock (1981) defined qualitative research as research that describes the subject under study in terms of its qualities without reducing these to numbers. Hancock further noted that qualitative research approaches are particularly well suited to areas of inquiry in which little is known. The qualitative approach is especially important to the present study, since it focuses on a prevalent but unstudied societal problem.

31

Black Grandparents As Parents

Strauss and Corbin (1990) stated that qualitative research is done by researchers in the social and behavioral sciences, and also by practitioners in fields that concern themselves with issues related to human behavior and functioning. According to these authors, qualitative analysis is fundamentally "any kind of research that produces findings not arrived at by means of statistical procedures or other means of quantification" (p. 17). They further note that these non-mathematical procedures result in findings by means of participant-observation and interviews as well as documents, books, videotapes, and quantitative data such as the census, among other sources. Similar procedures are also used by clinical psychologists when they base their conclusions primarily on nonverbal behavior (Strauss, 1987).

The Grounded Theory Method of Qualitative Analysis. The methodological thrust of grounded theory is a style of doing qualitative analysis that includes theoretical sampling and certain methodological guidelines, such as making constant comparisons and using a coding paradigm (Strauss, 1967; Schatzman & Strauss, 1973; Glaser, 1978). The mode of qualitative analysis for the present study was grounded theory. Blumer (1969) stated that the use of a theoretical approach in identifying relationships in human experiences most often draws from descriptive accounts, direct observations, life histories, and field studies. This approach, Blumer argued, forms a body of relevant observations about how people understand and accept their world and their actions and relationships within it. The value of the grandparents' experiences as they parent their grandchildren depends on the researcher's ability to remain sensitive to the process by which the respondents organize and give meaning to their perceptions and experiences.

Methods

Glaser and Strauss (1969) developed the grounded theory approach. According to these authors, this approach is grounded in the data. The grounded theory style of analysis is based on the premise that theory at various levels of generality is indispensable for deeper knowledge of social phenomena (Glaser & Strauss, 1967; Glaser, 1978). Strauss (1987) noted that the grounded theory methodology emphasizes the need for developing many concepts and their linkages. These linkages should characterize the central phenomenon that is studied during any research project.

Charmaz (1990) noted that grounded theorists use emerging theoretical categories to shape the data collection while in the field as well as to structure the analytic processes of coding and memo-making. Charmaz further noted that grounded theorists usually begin their study with general research questions despite a common perception that the inductive method begins with a clean slate.

The general procedure of grounded theory that I used in the present study was the systematic coding and comparing of the data to produce well-constructed theory (Strauss, 1987). The general elements of the main procedures were:

1. *Themes.* From my observations of the members of the GAP support group, I noted certain themes that recurred in their discussions of their experiences. I used these themes to prepare my questions for the one-on-one interviews.

2. *Interviews.* I conducted one-on-one interviews with fourteen grandparents who had been parenting their grandchildren for a minimum of two years. I used fifteen research questions to guide the grandparents into talking comfortably and openly about their experiences.

3. *Coding.* I audiotaped the interviews, had the tapes professionally transcribed, and then I coded the transcriptions line-by-line for important themes. Strauss (1987) noted that while coding involves the discovery and naming of categories, the aim is to produce concepts that seem to fit the data.

4. *Core categories.* Core categories emerged from these findings and served as preliminary organizing themes. Through line-by-line coding of each interview, I identified various themes. These included: (a) the grandparents' loss of significant expectations at this stage of their lives; (b) their feelings of deprivation of both normal and expected relationships with their own children; (c) their fears about whether their grandchildren would be normal and healthy; (d) their feelings of ambivalence as they struggled with their love for their own children and their angry feelings toward them for their drug addiction; and (e) their financial burdens as they took on the role of surrogate parents to their grandchildren.

5. *Theoretical sampling.* I tested emerging concepts for validity in the GAP support group meetings.

6. *Constant comparisons.* Through memo-writing in which I made comparisons of each grandparent's experience, I noted that the grandparents shared similar experiences in both the interviews and the GAP support group meetings. For example, in both settings they all identified major losses and adjustments as they took on the parenting roles of their grandchildren.

7. *Theoretical saturation.* I scrutinized the data to include all possible variations on themes, no matter how unique.

8. *Integration of the theory.* In transferring the identified codes to concepts, I found that these grandparents identified actual feelings

during the one-on-one interviews as well as in the GAP support group meetings. I identified the codes of ill health and financial burdens as concepts of major losses.

9. *Theoretical memos*. From the themes identified on 2" x 5" color-coded cards, I wrote memos. Strauss (1987) noted that writing memos helps the researcher to gain analytical distance from the material. The memos further assist the researcher's movement away from the data to abstract thinking, after which the researcher can return to the data to ground the abstractions in reality.

10. *Theoretical sorting*. Memos facilitated my sorting of theories to create a logic to the presentation. This is an essential process that cannot be skipped (Glaser, 1978).

Because this area of inquiry is largely understudied, I employed qualitative methods as a tool for discovery. In the process of an emerging complex set of relationships between the respondents and me, I used several unique methods in the field research. These included participant-observation, clinical interviews, and social actions. I subjected the collected data to the grounded theory method of qualitative analysis. In that process, new knowledge about the study group emerged.

3

Results

Introduction

Analyzing the data illuminated my understanding of the experiences of these grandparents who parent their grandchildren. What I found were variations in the contexts and consequences of these experiences and a broad spectrum of differences in the grandparents' responses.

All of the grandparents traveled this uncharted journey through a period of increasing awareness, during which both feelings of self-blame and betrayal were awakened. They all shouldered this burden in unique ways. This involved dealing with feelings of ambivalence about taken-for-granted emotions, adjustments within the family structure and relationships, and coping with this new challenge at a time in their lives when they had other expectations for themselves.

The consequences of this disruption were traumatic. While there were certainly possible gains for the emotional lives of some, in the main the consequences for most were negative and characterized by serious losses. The most important of these losses included the grandparents'

Results

future goals, their traditional social life, their expected leisure diver-
sions, their anticipated independence accompanying an empty nest,
their perceived physical health, and their financial status.

Awareness of Child's Drug Use

The awareness of their children's involvement with drugs was
experienced by these grandparents in different ways. However, common to most of them is a concept of self and family that is highly
idealized. They define the ideal family as one in which everyone goes
to church, and the children attend Sunday School and are good students
with no social behavior or academic problems in school. The grandparents further believe that family members should have frequent gather-
ings in which parents and children have close relationships with open
lines of communication. By this ethic, as one grandmother said, "good
families do not produce bad children."

As these grandparents describe their close supportive relationships
with their children, they indicate that their awareness of their children's
drug involvement and/or addiction resulted in them feeling deceived
and betrayed by their children, thus compounding the rupture of family
ties. This perceived deception causes grandparents to feel physically
and emotionally devastated. One grandparent indicated that the awareness of her daughter's drug addiction was one of the most terrible times
in her life. She described feeling as if the addiction amounted to a death
in her family, and she indicated that there has been no way for her to
recover from her emotional pain. Several grandparents report that they
are still trying to accept the emotional loss of their adult children to

drugs, even as they take on the responsibilities of parenting their grandchildren.

Two common ways that grandparents described their feelings as they became aware of their children's drug addiction were self-blame and betrayal.

Self-Blame. Within the present study, the grandparents who tended to blame themselves differed from the grandparents who experienced a sense of betrayal from their children in that the former recognized early their child's involvement in drugs. Actual awareness of their child's cocaine addiction was preceded by their child's suspicious behaviors, which, when later reviewed, were recognized as indicators of drug activities. Although grandparents recognized the drug involvement, they initially denied that this could be happening in their family. They felt that in parenting their own children, they had provided an ideal home for them.

Grandparents who experience self-blame for their child's drug addiction tend to review the past repeatedly. They obsess about where they might have gone wrong and why they didn't acknowledge the problems earlier. One grandparent stated, "When my daughter was a little girl, she began running away from home. She was getting in bad company with hardheaded, disobedient children. She would sneak out at night even if she got punished for her behavior. I feel she was under peer pressure." According to this grandparent, when her daughter entered junior high school, she began staying out late at night and away from home for several days at a time. She dropped out of school and became pregnant when she was fifteen. At this point, the grandparent began to acknowledge that something must be wrong. But despite her

Results

suspicions that her daughter was involved in drugs, she continued to deny that this could be happening to her daughter. Because of the early onset of her daughter's behaviors, the grandparent blames herself for not attempting to do more to protect her daughter from drugs.

A number of grandparents in the present study felt guilty because they did not respond to early signs of their children's addictive behaviors. They blame themselves for not acknowledging early indicators that signaled problems. These grandparents now feel that if they had acknowledged the existence of the deviant behaviors, they might have been able to provide more positive direction and guidance for their children.

One grandparent reported that her daughter began having social behavioral problems at school at an early age. She began cutting school, cutting classes, and spending time in the park with her friends. According to the grandparent, her daughter began isolating herself from family members and displaying oppositional behaviors within the family. This grandparent stated, "When I talked with my daughter about my feelings and concerns, my daughter assured me nothing was wrong and that I was just being square and too rigid. I then began to feel that perhaps I was overreacting, and as long as my daughter respected me, I would not worry." This grandparent indicated that, at this point, she was too afraid to acknowledge the likelihood of her daughter's drug problem.

Grandparents react to their feelings of self-blame in different ways. Some of them attempt to rationalize their past parenting style, some of them feel guilty about their children's chosen behavior, or they become overprotective of their grandchildren. Ignorance about drugs is one of their rationalizations for their failure to recognize and deal with their child's addiction. For example, Ms. B. stated:

Black Grandparents As Parents

> My daughter and I were such good friends. We were very
> close. Even though I observed some early troublesome signs
> of problems with my daughter, I denied everything. When
> she began using the white powder, I think she called it crank,
> she even offered me some to put in my coffee. She told me
> if I put a little of this in my coffee, I can lose weight. She
> assured me this was not addictive, and it was the same thing
> diet pills are made of.

This grandparent described feeling shocked and not wanting to believe
that one of her children would get hooked on "dope." She accepted her
daughter's explanation with some reservation.

Ms. R. stated, "A lot of this, I think, is my fault. Maybe if I had
recognized and acknowledged the problems earlier, I could have helped
my daughter." Another grandparent blames herself because she feels
that she and her husband didn't tell their daughter often enough that they
loved her and that she was a pretty girl. Many grandparents report that
the knowledge of their adult children's drug addiction resulted in the
entire family feeling so embarrassed that they couldn't talk to anyone
about the drug problem. The entire family seemed to feel a responsibility for the drug addiction of one of its family members. One grandparent
stated:

> The awareness of our daughter's drug addiction was so
> painful and embarrassing to the whole family that we chose
> not to talk to anyone about what was going on in our family.
> We felt our family would be judged by our daughter's drug
> behavior. We felt alone, sad, and embarrassed because of
> what had happened to our family.

In some instances, grandparents deal with their self-blame for their
children's drug addiction by being overprotective of their grandchildren. They appear to be focusing on safe parenting and protection of

their grandchildren, as they are convinced that their grandchildren need them. They want to make sure that they are there for them. In the process, they also distance themselves from their own children. One grandparent stated, "I'm so afraid that my grandchildren will follow their parents' footsteps. This would kill me. I know my grandchildren need me. I'm trying to do it right this time, and I try not to take anything for granted."

Many grandparents feel that they must protect their grandchildren from the malignant environment that influenced their drug-addicted children. They fear that their grandchildren might repeat the drug behavior of their parents. One grandparent reported, "I feel lost. I don't know where I'm going. I think I was a pretty strict parent, but very fair. I'm just trying to do a better job of parenting my grandchildren." These grandparents are fervently observant of their grandchildren's behaviors and activities and concerned with their environment and future. One grandparent reported, "I've already started thinking about a good junior high school for my five-year-old grandson. I want to make sure that he is in a safe school environment as he grows older." Another grandparent stated:

> I just want to make sure that each of my grandchildren gets a good education. That's the bottom line. I try to keep them involved in positive and meaningful activities. I don't let them go to the park alone. I'm too afraid what might happen. If I can't take them, I just let them play outside. I'm very concerned about them.

Sense of Betrayal. By contrast, grandparents who mainly feel betrayed had experienced no prior knowledge or evidence of their children's drug activity. In many instances, the grandparents were motivated to deny the drug activity of their adult children. According to one grandparent:

Black Grandparents As Parents

> Our family has always been so close. We always did things
> together, like have dinners, and would get together for
> holidays and birthdays. We always had so much fun. My
> daughter was the life of the party. She never missed being
> with the family. Then, all at once, we didn't see her. She
> began drifting away from the family. She was on drugs for
> a year, and I didn't know it. I thought she was working,
> because she was working two jobs. I just sit and think, "Why
> did this have to happen?" I just sit and spin with the pain.

According to this grandparent, there were no early signs or clues that this daughter had a drug habit.

In some instances, the grandparents' awareness of their children's drug problem results in the grandparents having to immediately take on the parenting role of their grandchildren. A paternal grandmother who took on the parenting responsibility of her infant grandson indicated that she thought it would be a temporary arrangement. The baby was born four months premature and was abandoned in the hospital by its mother. Because this 1-pound, 11-ounce baby was born "crack"-exposed, he was very sick and remained in the hospital four months after birth. The biological father agreed to take this child once he had recovered from his own drug-related "illness." According to the grandmother, it has now been three years, and she still has her grandchild. This grandmother expressed feeling angry, betrayed, punished, and "put upon" by her son. She reported having no awareness of her son's drug addiction. He had previously been close with his family and had never caused her any behavioral problems. He was a good student in school and was an honor student who never got involved in any trouble. The grandmother felt betrayed by her son because, before now, she had never had any reason *not* to trust him.

Results

Mr. D. reported:

> I only have one daughter, and I love her dearly. I gave my
> daughter everything but my life. I put her in college, or at
> least I *thought* she was in college. After my grandbaby was
> born, we would frequently keep her on weekends to give our
> daughter a break and because we loved our grandbaby. One
> weekend, as we were preparing to return our grandbaby, our
> daughter called and asked us not to bring the grandbaby
> home but take her to a friend's house. We were not suspi-
> cious about this because we just thought our daughter was
> late returning from wherever she was and had made arrange-
> ments for her baby. However, soon after that, our daughter
> began dropping the grandbaby off at our home instead of us
> picking the grandbaby up at *her* home. We arrived unexpect-
> edly at our daughter's home one day. We noticed our
> daughter behaving strangely, and she would not invite us
> into her home. We finally went inside and observed suspi-
> cious cigarette butts [marijuana] in the ashtray. We again
> refused to believe this had anything to do with our daughter,
> hoping that someone else had left the cigarette butts there.
> Finally, on another unexpected visit to our daughter's home,
> we noticed burn marks and bruises on our grandbaby's body.
> Our daughter's apartment was totally bare of furniture. We
> took our grandbaby home with us, and our daughter has
> never come for her. That was eight years ago, and we now
> have two of our grandchildren. We don't know where our
> daughter is.

While grandparents deal with feeling betrayed by their children's
drug addiction, they also feel confused as to how to handle the disruption
and loss of trust in their relationship with their children. They are
parenting their grandchildren and feel angry and resentful toward their
own children. One grandmother indicated that her daughter, whom she
has always trusted and been very close to, has stolen so much from her
to support her drug addiction that the grandmother became confused
about whether she really had certain things (clothes, money, small

appliances), continuing to refuse to believe that her daughter would steal from her. This grandmother reported:

> Because I feel so betrayed by my daughter, whom I have always trusted, I just don't know how to deal with my feelings toward her. I know I should love my daughter and be civil toward her, but it's hard to deal with my anger and resentment toward her because of what she has done to me. I still try to put my feelings aside and love her. I really want to trust her each time I think she is getting better. But each time I feel I can trust her, she betrays my trust again.

Sometimes grandparents' feelings of anger and embarrassment over the drug involvement of their children actually overrides any sense of obligation toward parenting their grandchildren. While this attitude was only voiced by slightly more than one-fourth of the grandparents in the present study, it is a powerful indication of the extent of their anger and grief. These were all grandparents who felt betrayed by their children's drug addiction. As they work through their feelings of being punished and "put upon" by their children, some have decided to return their grandchildren to their parents and allow the social-service system to intervene, perhaps placing the grandchildren in foster placement. For a variety of reasons, these grandparents feel a need to relinquish the responsibility of being "parents" to their grandchildren, although this is a decision fraught with ambivalence and inner conflict driven by their feelings of resentment.

Sometimes this decision is made when the intrusion and disrespect of the drug-involved children have resulted in the grandchildren expressing divided loyalty and love for their parents and their grandparents. One fifty-year-old grandmother stated:

Results

> I need to save myself from all the strain and stress of
> parenting my grandchildren. At this point in my life, I must
> make decisions for myself. My grandchildren continue to
> emotionally abuse me because they are angry with their
> parents for not being with them. I feel I need to make a choice
> between my health and continuing to raise my grandchil-
> dren. I realize that I am the most important person in my
> grandchildren's life. I love my grandchildren, but I feel that
> I need to heal. I feel I need to find a way to put my
> grandchildren back with their parents. I'm too old, and I'm
> tired. Letting go of my grandchildren will be difficult for me.

The above examples illustrate the grandparents' feelings of betrayal over their children's drug addiction. Because some of the grandparents believed that they had a "good" and "close" family, they tended to deny the existence of their children's drug addiction to protect their image of the family. One grandmother stated:

> I'm very embarrassed about the exposure of my family
> because of my daughter's drug activities and having to
> parent my grandchildren. I really feel betrayed by my
> daughter because I really trusted her. At times, I don't want
> to talk to anyone about my grandchildren, so I immediately
> pull back. I'm very embarrassed that my daughter uses
> drugs. We try to keep her away from our friends so that no
> one will see her. We all feel betrayed by her because we all
> love her.

Summary. In brief, some grandparents primarily feel guilty and some grandparents primarily feel betrayed by their adult children's drug addiction. Those grandparents who feel guilty or blame themselves for their children's drug behavior deal with their experiences by either rationalizing their feelings or becoming overprotective of their grand- children. They feel that the parenting of their grandchildren gives them

45

a chance to do it right this time. A small portion of those grandparents who feel betrayed by their adult children's drug behavior are inclined to return their grandchildren to their parents. They are more likely to attempt to recapture their lives, which they had put on hold as they took on the parenting needs of their grandchildren. In both situations, there are significant adjustments within the family as family units are redefined—in many instances, to include multigenerational arrangements.

Shouldering the Burden

Feelings of Obligations. After the decision to take on the responsibility of parenting their grandchildren, grandparents display a variety of concerns. They ask, "What are we raising these grandchildren to be? Are we raising another generation of drug addicts?" One of the burdens for them is the loss of their family continuity. Another difficulty in adjustment is the bitterness they feel over being taken advantage of by their children. Yet another problem is the loss of their positive self-image as good parents. They describe feeling used as pawns by their own children.

Initially, according to the grandparents, they took on the parenting responsibilities of their grandchildren because they felt obligated to do so. Among the reasons they give for taking on this responsibility is the impression from the social-service system that they had no choice in the circumstances. One grandparent reports that because her daughter was addicted to "crack," she had abandoned her $2\frac{1}{2}$-month-old baby in a vacant apartment. According to the grandparent:

Results

> My daughter left this baby alone in this apartment while she
> went looking for drugs. I was called by the police and told
> that they were taking my grandbaby to foster placement
> unless I could come and take the baby. I felt that I had no
> choice. I didn't want my grandbaby to be placed with
> strangers. I felt a sense of obligation to my grandbaby and my
> family. I have had my grandbaby since then, and he is three
> years old now.

It was only after the grandparents realized that their grandchildren
were being abandoned, neglected, and abused by their parents that they
began to feel an emotional obligation to the children. Some of them
indicated that at the initial phase of learning about their adult children's
drug addiction, they had refused to take care of their grandchildren. One
grandmother reported that her grandchild had been born and abandoned
in the hospital. She was called by the Department of Social Services
(DSS) and asked to take this grandchild, who was reported to be quite
ill because of prenatal drug exposure. This grandparent reported feeling
both angry and confused. She indicated that she refused to see her
grandchild because she felt that if she saw the child she couldn't refuse
to take her. The grandparent stated:

> I just can't see how I can deal with a sick grandbaby right
> now. I do plan to visit my grandbaby in the hospital, but I feel
> so afraid, angry, and confused. I have to deal with that. I'm
> trying to get my life together after raising my own five
> children. My husband just died, and I have to work.

Many of these grandparents also describe feeling concerned and
worried about their grandchildren's family identity if they are placed in
foster placement with nonrelatives. Some believe that, years later, their
grandchildren will attempt to find out their actual identity and the
location of their blood relatives. Grandparents feel concerned that,

should their grandchildren be put in foster placement, they will question the absence of their biological family and wonder why nobody in their family wanted them. One grandmother reported:

> I almost let Child Protective Services [CPS] take my grand-
> child on off, but then all I could see is, maybe within five or
> more years, my grandchild trying to figure out who she is and
> where is her family. I would feel so guilty that I just couldn't
> live with myself.

Another major concern for some of these grandmothers is the feeling that their children have turned them from being loving grandparents into "angry and resentful old women." They are concerned about the loss of the positive image they expected would accompany their grandparent role, and they feel stuck with this negative label.

As they approach retirement age, these grandparents feel taken advantage of by their children as they deal with the demands of the total parenting responsibility for their grandchildren. Ms. R. indicated, "My family don't seem to care how many kids they poke on me. I guess because I'm a person who don't say no, they take advantage of me." Grandparents feel deprived of their leisure time to do things they enjoy and had looked forward to doing once they had completed the parenting of their own children. All the grandparents talk about how they love their grandchildren, even the ones who are now planning to return the children to their parents. As a rule, they all feel overwhelmed by the role of primary caretaker for their grandchildren. One grandmother stated:

> I'm too old, I'm too tired. I'm an old, single grandparent. I've
> been parenting my grandchildren for seventeen years. It has
> been very difficult for me. Sometimes I just don't see any
> logic in this. It is difficult for me to keep up with the demands

of parenting my grandchildren. I'm seventy years old, and I'm tired.

These grandparents are attempting to provide stable lives for their grandchildren, who may never have known what stability is. One grandparent asked:

> How do we discipline or punish these grandchildren for their inappropriate behaviors when they already feel punished? Because of our role of raising our grandchildren, we have been turned from loving grandparents to mean old ladies.

Most poignant of all is that everyone involved is dealing with personal losses and traumas. The grandchildren are separated from their parents, often not knowing when they will see them again, or perhaps not understanding why they cannot be with their parents. The grandparents are besieged with feelings of failure about their own adult children's outcomes. They feel angry at the adults' irresponsibility or inability to parent their children. And the parents, addicted to drugs, no doubt have their own traumas and losses, from which they seek to escape.

Feelings of Ambivalence. In spite of the love that these grandparents have for their sons and daughters, they have expressed feelings of ambivalence as they attempt to separate their love for their adult children from the latter's drug problems. They still love their children and find it difficult to let go of them, even though they feel betrayed and punished by them. They feel torn and confused as they attempt to acknowledge their feelings of anger and resentment toward their children. Many of the grandparents attempt to deal with these ambivalent feelings toward their adult children by being overly attached to and/or overly protective of their grandchildren. Despite the grandparents' ambivalence, however, their loving feelings frequently prevail. One grandmother reported, "As much as I love my daughter, it is hard for me to love and own my daughter and disown her drug problems."

Many of these grandparents feel that "there has to be a better way" of taking care of their grandchildren and achieving a satisfying life for themselves. They feel torn by their hopes for themselves and their concerns for their family. One grandparent indicated, "As I took on the parenting responsibilities of my grandchildren, I felt grief-stricken, just dead inside, because I felt I had no choice in this situation. I feel that this was forced on me, and I felt committed to my grandchildren." This sense of commitment has forced the grandparents to revise and revamp their lives in their later adult developmental stages.

Some grandparents described feeling as if they were "fighting Satan" as they attempted to deal with the complex issues and concerns around the drug addiction of their children. One grandmother stated:

> My daughter has had so many starts. We have helped her so many times in whatever ways we could, including giving her emotional support and encouragement. I feel angry and resentful at times. There are times I actually feel that I hate my daughter, even though I know that I still love her.

Ms. R. reported:

> I feel very angry with my daughter because she stole my child away from me. I had to cut her off. This is the child that I birthed, that I loved, that I took care of, and that I sacrificed for. She was mine then. I felt that I was in full control. When she got in control, she went her way. That's the part I hate. I never lost my daughter. I lost a woman. I lost a woman which I couldn't deal with. That makes me angry.

Results

Another grandmother stated:

> I love both of my daughters, but I can't stand them. I have lost both of my daughters to "crack" cocaine. I am having a difficult time letting go of my daughters. I am trying to heal my feelings and deny that I love them. I know I love them, because they are my daughters regardless of what's happening to them now. They made this choice. They know that I will help them if they would only come to me.

In summary, the grandparents in the present study tended to feel ambivalent, with a sense of obligation, as they took on the parenting of their grandchildren. They indicated that, because of the close ties of their family, and also to protect the family identity for their grandchildren, they were reluctant to allow the children to be placed in foster placement with nonrelatives. Many of these grandparents expressed feeling disappointed and angry with their own adult children on account of the latter's drug addiction. They feel that their children could have made better choices for themselves, and they feel angry with themselves for their own role in permitting this to happen.

Adjustments Within the Family. Taking on the parenting of their grandchildren has forced major adjustments in the lives of all the grandparents in this study. Some of these adjustments have included: moving to larger and more appropriate living space to accommodate the grandchildren; purchasing needed furniture (especially baby beds); adjusting work schedules; locating babysitters or child-care facilities; making arrangements for school enrollment; assuming responsibility for school attendance, homework, and other school-related activities; and providing transportation for the children. One grandmother who is parenting four grandchildren, ranging in age from two to nineteen, stated:

> When I took on the parenting of my grandchildren, I was living in a one-bedroom apartment. I had one bed, which was my bed. Once my grandchildren came to live with me, we all had to sleep in this one bedroom and bed. I had a smaller room which I was using as a storage room because it was too small for a bedroom. After I had raised my own children, I moved to a smaller apartment and decorated it just for me. It was very hard and difficult for me at first to make this adjustment in my life. I had to find furniture for my grandchildren and readjust my work schedule plus my whole life.

Another grandmother reported:

> Before I began parenting my grandchildren, I carpooled to work with other ladies. I only had myself to take care of. All I had to do was just be ready when they came. Or if it was my turn to drive, I just drove to get them and didn't have anything else to worry about. Since I began parenting my grandchildren, I'm no longer able to ride with anyone, because I have to make special arrangements for my grandchildren. I have to take them to babysitters or pick them up after work. This is a big adjustment for me.

How These Grandparents Cope. Grandparents' coping strategies for dealing with these stresses involve several approaches. As mentioned earlier, some of these grandparents, especially the single ones, see themselves as single moms raising their grandchildren in a dysfunctional family.

Coping often includes both using personal resources and reaching out to community agencies. Many grandparents initially deal with their feelings by crying in private and denying what is happening to their family. Some told me that they cried so much at first that they no longer have any tears. Others just walk and cry with every step they take. One way to overcome their sorrow is to reminisce—for example, by looking at old pictures of the family when the children were young and everyone seemed happy. Some grandparents, however, take to alcohol or food to dull their grief.

When grandparents do reach beyond the privacy of their home, community agencies play an important role in helping them to cope. An important resource is a strong alliance with members of their church congregation. Some grandparents pray often and read scriptures from the Bible, trusting that God will remove their burdens from them. Their spiritual resources provide them with comfort and solace in private as well as in church.

These grandparents search for positive male role models for their grandsons. They look for male family members and neighbors, as well as reaching out to child-serving agencies such as local fraternities and "Big Brother" organizations. Child-care is available for their preschool grandchildren through Bananas, Inc., in Oakland. Since all grandparents for this study were recruited through Bananas, all respondents were affiliated with that organization.

Psychotherapy is a resource for both the grandchildren and the grandparents. Some grandparents seek psychotherapy for their grandchildren to assist them in dealing with their feelings of being abandoned by their parents. There are also many psychosocial, school-related problems, some of which are associated with the children being parented by their grandparents. Many of these grandchildren feel isolated from their peer group, or they deliberately isolate themselves, because they feel embarrassed when there are planned school activities for parents and children, since these force them to admit that they live with their grandparents. One grandparent indicated that her grandchildren refuse to tell her about planned family activities at school because they don't want to go with their grandparents.

Many grandparents seek psychotherapy for themselves to deal with the stresses around parenting their grandchildren and coping with the drug addiction of their own adult children. Social support groups, such as the Grandparents As Parents (GAP) support group that was organized by Bananas, have provided an emotional outlet for these grandparents where they can feel comfortable and secure in an environment that accepts their pain.

Grandparents who attend the GAP support group have often benefited from the positive alliances they form with other grandparents who share similar experiences. A number of these grandparents have formed "mini-supports" within the group. They frequently call each other to offer emotional support. They form car pools to and from the GAP support group. They assist each other in transportation to and from medical appointments. They go out to local restaurants for dinner. However, they are careful to set limits for themselves, such as not babysitting each other's grandchildren. Already overloaded with the responsibilities of parenting their own grandchildren, they want, in this context, to limit themselves to adult interactions.

Consequences

When grandparents take on the responsibility of parenting their grandchildren, there are important consequences that they experience

54

during this process. There are gains and there are losses involved in the caretaking of their grandchildren.

Gains. Grandparents who have been parenting their grandchildren for two or more years and do not plan to return the children to their parents or to other agencies tend to feel that the children are their reconstituted family. In their effort to cope with this adjustment in their lives, they attempt to recapture earlier issues of parenting their own children. Ms. B. indicated, "There is very little in life that is all bad. Having my grandchildren has its upside too. I feel that we are a family now. They keep me going and connected with the world of children."

Although the grandparents I interviewed said little about the unanticipated gains of parenting their grandchildren, they have attempted to find some pleasures in their new responsibilities. Ms. A. stated, "Parenting my grandchildren can be an advantage for me in just being around them and getting to know them. I enjoy them. They are company for me." Ms. R. stated:

> Having my grandchildren gives me strength. Due to my illness [multiple sclerosis], I can't tell, if I was not sick with MS, what it would be like. I don't know where I'd be. Because of my illness, parenting my grandchildren gives me a cause to wake up in the morning. To do things, to move. I feel I have no choice. Whereas being sick and just being by myself, I would probably stay in bed. Having my grandchildren keeps me involved in something. I do enjoy being involved with them, even though it gets difficult at times.

These grandparents feel a sense of obligation to their grandchildren. They are concerned about the children's physical and emotional health and well-being. They plan future goals and directions for them. Some grandparents report that there is joy in their new role as parents of their grandchildren. They feel that their grandchildren are there for them— that they have someone to talk to, someone to help keep their faith strong. One grandparent indicated that when she gets old and sick, her grandchildren may be the only ones to take care of her and keep her from being placed in a rest home. They will be "there" for her just as she is presently "here" for them.

Losses. While many of the grandparents I interviewed acknowledged gains from having parenting responsibilities for their grandchildren, most of them focused on losses. Some of the losses result from the direct effects of the new demands on the grandparents' lives, as indicated earlier. However, other losses are self-imposed, due to the impact of social and psychological perceptions of stigma and shame on the grandparents' personal and family identities. It was often unclear from the grandparents' reports which kind of loss was more influential in changing their lives. They weighed and balanced their self-interests with the interests of their grandchildren and other family members. Therefore, losses could be attributed to a combination of objective circumstances and subjective states of mind. Objective circumstances were conditions over which the grandparents had no control. These include their own aging process, their economic situation, and the organization of social services. Subjective states of mind for these grandparents have to do with their emotional responses to the conditions of their life. These include the grandparents' self-image, their ego strength, their self-esteem, and their reaction to stigmas or negative labels that they experience as they assume the primary parenting responsibilities for their grandchildren.

Results

The main losses with which the grandparents were concerned include:

1. Loss of future goals
2. Loss of social life
3. Loss of leisure
4. Loss of independence
5. Loss of physical health
6. Financial burdens

Each of these concerns is discussed below.

Loss of Future Goals. For all of the grandparents, the disruption of the continuity of their goals or outlets left them feeling angry and deprived. Four patterns of loss of future goals emerged from reports by these grandparents: (a) those with the most positive attitudes sought to reconnect with the threads of goals and sense of self from their former lives; (b) others felt that their lives were "put on hold"; (c) some felt a sense of deprivation; and (d) the most negative expressions were feelings of total relinquishment of their lives' direction and total abandonment of their sense of self.

Reconnecting with their goals. After an initial period of adjustment to their new parenting role, some grandparents feel that they would like to reconnect with portions of their lives that have been interrupted. For example, they may have ambitions to resume their previous plans. The early parenting process required their focus on issues relating to the needs and adjustments of the children, but now some grandparents can resume planning for themselves and accommodating their own needs. Often their plans had been set into action before this change in their lives. These goals were integral to their past selves. Other goals were expressed wishes that had never been acted upon and now probably never will be.

Ms. R. reported that ten years ago she had been placed on medical disability from her job. "I had returned to school," she said, "and had begun taking classes at a local junior college. Six years ago, I took on the responsibility of parenting my grandchildren. Because of this responsibility, I had to give up all my future goals. Who knows? Maybe after my grandchildren are grown, I might finish my goals."

Ms. W. indicated that before she began parenting her grandchildren, she had received a job promotion. She had returned to school to receive additional training for her new position. Once she began parenting her grandchildren, however, she had to give up her job promotion and return to her former position because she was not able to continue her training while parenting two small children. Nevertheless, Ms. W. stated, "I feel that even though I am not able to continue my training for a new job, once my grandchildren are grown and able to take care of themselves, I plan to go back to school if I'm not too old and tired."

In spite of the major adjustments that this subset of grandparents are making as they parent their grandchildren, they still feel optimistic about regaining control of their lives. Ms. E. said:

> I have a computer background. I've even dabbled in pro-
> gramming a little. I've always done mentally stimulating
> things. I work crossword puzzles and read a lot. My goal is
> to help my daughter recover and get her life together, so that
> she can take her child, so that I can ride off in the sunset and
> complete my goals in life.

Results

Another grandparent stated:

> I have always been interested in playing the piano. I have become an amateur piano player, which I enjoy very much. I had hoped to continue my training in piano. I am also going back to school to complete my training in mental health. Once I began parenting my grandchild, it has been difficult for me to find sufficient time to practice the piano and also to study and keep up with my schoolwork. I am, however, continuing my school. I still hope that I can return to my piano lessons. I hope things will work out for me. I feel, at times, that this is not right—that this was not meant to be. This is difficult for me, but I still feel positive that I will somehow get to finish my goals.

These wished-for goals were integral to the grandparents' present sense of self. Even though these grandparents feel that their goals have been temporarily disrupted or delayed, they seem to have some hope of resuming their prior plans.

Lives put on hold. Some grandparents did not foresee a future when their goals could be reclaimed. Their responses suggest a sense of personal displacement rather than readjustment, and they can't seem to get on with their lives. They feel stuck.

Many of these grandparents feel that they are "back to square one" as parents—that is, they have had children, they have raised children, they have launched their children, and now they suddenly find themselves having to raise children all over again. This places the grandparents in a seemingly no-win situation—a position of cycling and recycling the same stages of their adult lives. Ms. D. explained that since she has raised her own six children, who are all now grown, there are things

59

in her life that she has never been able to do because she had children. She indicated that when she was parenting her own children, she took care of them and sacrificed many things in her life for them. Ms. R. stated, "My two children were grown. I felt grown because I was feeling that since my children were grown, now I can catch up with my life. Parenting my grandchildren has changed that."

These grandparents felt that they had put certain aspects of their life on hold the first time they parented. Now they are putting their lives on hold again. Such repeated cycling and recycling of the parenting stage of their lives make disappointments over unfulfilled dreams a prominent aspect of their present grief.

Deprivation. Feeling deprived seems to be a common theme among most of the grandparents as they perform the primary parenting responsibilities for their grandchildren. Ms. N. reported, "I feel deprived of doing things that I had really wanted to do. I was planning to return to school to receive training in an effort to make a career change. Once I began parenting my grandchild, my plans were interrupted. I still feel angry and resentful for this interruption in my life."

Feelings of deprivation resulted from spoiled expectations about how life would treat these grandparents in their older years. This sense of deprivation has resulted from grandparents having to give up meaningful directions in their own lives to accommodate the parenting needs of their grandchildren. Ms. J. stated:

> Both my husband and I are retired. We had planned to spend some time with our grandchildren. We did not expect to have them *all* the time. This is certainly different from what we had planned. We had planned to do lots of traveling and

spending time doing things that we wanted to do that did not
include children. We are parenting four of our grandchildren. This has caused a big adjustment for us.

Many of these grandparents also feel deprived of enjoying a more
typical grandparent-grandchild relationship, and they feel deprived of
a positive and loving relationship with their own adult children. Most
would agree with Ms. E., who stated:

> I just want to be a grandmother to my grandchild, so that I
> could do things with him which I really want to do and would
> enjoy doing as a grandparent. I have always looked forward
> to the day when I could enjoy being a grandparent. I don't
> want to be a parent to my grandchild. I feel deprived of
> having a happy and loving relationship with my daughter.

Ms. D. reported feeling deprived of social outlets as she parents her
four grandchildren. "I just wish that my daughter would get her life
together and get her kids," she said. "So help me, Lord, I will be glad for
her to get them. I need to enjoy this part of my life, away from parenting
children."

Grandparents with the strongest feelings of deprivation were most
likely to retain the goal of returning their grandchildren to their parents.
One of these grandparents stated:

> My intent always has been, and still is, that I can help my
> daughter get herself together. I will give her the emotional
> support and encouragement she needs to pull herself to-
> gether, so that she can take her son, hopefully before he's old
> enough to actually go to school. He is three years old now.
> I want to be a parent to my daughter, where we could do the
> things a mother and daughter like to do—bake, share recipes,
> shop, and just be together. I want to be a grandparent to my
> grandchild, so that I could spoil him, and when I get tired of

him, I could take him to his mother. Each of my visits with him would be a special time for both of us.

Another grandparent explained:

> I feel I need to find a way to put my grandchildren back with their mother. I'm too old to keep up with this responsibility. I'm tired. I'm concerned about my health. My grandchildren need younger parents who have more energy, more patience, and can do more things with them. I have medical problems, and I feel that I need to save myself. It is hard for me to make this decision. I've worked through the guilt feelings I had. At times my older grandchildren verbally abuse me, especially after they have seen their parents. I must make a decision between my health or continuing to parent my grandchildren.

Ms. W. stated, "It is so sad that, at our age, wherever we go, we have to take these young 'grandbabies' with us. We are old grandparents with young 'grandbabies.'"

When grandparents take on the responsibility of parenting their grandchildren, they often are forced to give up many of their goals that they considered appropriate for their developmental age and stage. One grandparent reported:

> At my age I should be doing things that I want to do. I should be enjoying my life with my friends. I feel angry and embarrassed sometimes when I can't do things or go places I want to do or go. I should be able to sleep all night without having to be up with crying babies. Before I took on the parenting of my grandchildren, I had furnished my house the way I wanted it, with my special crystal pieces and light-colored carpet. I had to give up all that after I began parenting my grandchildren. I feel that my feelings and needs are no longer important. I now realize that we grandparents are the most important person to ourselves.

Results

Total relinquishing of goals and abdication of self. A number of grandparents in this study felt that once they began parenting their grandchildren, their whole life was sacrificed. Threads with their previous life were totally broken. The responsibility of parenting their grandchildren resulted in irrevocable changes in their lives and their sense of self. "When I took on the parenting of my three grandchildren," said Ms. R., "I had to give up my life. I had to give up 'me' to take on this responsibility. My life didn't seem important anymore." These grandparents describe the parenting responsibility in later years as very difficult. "It's rough when you give up all your needs. It's very hard," said Ms. R. Some grandparents, like Ms. Z., describe the task of parenting their grandchildren as "a long journey—a long tunnel that doesn't seem to have a light at the end." For many, it is a hopeless path.

A number of these grandparents see little prospect of reclaiming former activities and directions in their lives. They feel and fear that there is no recovery for them at this stage in their life. "I am in my fifties," one grandparent said. "I know that whatever happens to me now will be with me. I know that whatever changes take place in my life now will be final." Another grandparent reported that when she had retired from work, she had begun to do some of the things she had long wanted and planned to do, such as visiting interesting places, getting involved in social activities, and spending time with her friends. "I've had my grandchildren for seven years," she said. "I feel so frustrated that I just sit home. My friends are always asking me what has happened to me, because they don't see me anymore. My whole life has changed."

Ms. B. stated:

> I love my grandchildren dearly, but this has changed my
> entire life. I was running an office, getting ready to retire. I

was dabbling with photography. I had planned to travel. My plans were entirely canceled. I haven't been able to complete any of my plans.

In summary, most grandparents feel uncertain and pessimistic about how this interruption in their lives will affect their future goals. They are uncertain whether the interruption is temporary or permanent. Some confess that when they began parenting their grandchildren, they did not expect that it would stretch out this long. Grandparents who thought the interruption was temporary believed that they could recapture their goals. Those who viewed the parenting of their grandchildren as permanent felt that their lives had been permanently changed and saw little hope of recovering from the experience.

Loss of Social Life. Many of the grandparents curtailed some of their social activities as they took on the parenting of their grandchildren. Some did so voluntarily, others were torn and conflicted, and others felt shunned and excluded. Ms. J. stated:

> We definitely had to curtail some of our social activities. We were into the Masonics and other social activities and organizations before we began parenting our four grandchildren. My husband and I are both retired after working for so many years. We had travel and social plans that did not involve children. Because of this responsibility, we have had to give up many of our plans. I'm trying not to be angry, because it could be worse.

One example of a grandparent who had conflicted desires was Ms. D., who said:

> I still have contact with some of my high-school friends, but they are not raising their grandchildren. I would like to travel

and do things with them, but I feel embarrassed that when we plan things together, I have to cancel sometimes because I don't have arrangements for my grandchildren. My friends have even encouraged me to put my grandchildren in foster placements. I just couldn't live with myself if I did that. There are times when I feel so angry and confused that I ask myself, "What's in this for me?"

A common experience of these grandparents is feeling torn and conflicted by the social and emotional isolation from their peer group. One grandparent stated:

I no longer have the friends I once had, because they are all doing the things we had planned to do—travel, become involved in social activities, live our adult lives as we choose. Because I have my grandbaby, my friends seem to avoid me for fear I may ask them to babysit for me. They don't call me, or if I call them, they frequently will tell me they are planning to do things or are already busy. I feel totally isolated and abandoned by my friends. They seem afraid to call me.

Ms. M. reported that she was once frequently invited to adult social functions and activities with her friends, but now she is often unable to be with them because she has her grandson and no one to care for him. Ms. M. indicated that her friends no longer call or include her in their activities. This grandmother feels angry and frustrated by this isolation, but she feels that she has no other choice than to take care of her grandson.

Some grandparents feel excluded from social activities that are common and appropriate for their age group. According to Ms. M., "I have no social life. I go to church. I walk through the door and back through the door. I feel I have no place to go." While some of these grandparents are indeed abandoned by their friends and family because of perceived pressures or stigmas, they also isolate themselves because of these things. Many feel uncomfortable admitting to their peers the real reasons they are parenting their grandchildren. One grandparent reported:

> We belong to some of the same social groups, we are members of the same church. We are afraid that if we told our friends that we are parenting our grandchildren because our daughter is addicted to "crack" cocaine, our whole family would be judged. That is too painful. This is embarrassing and painful for our family.

Another grandparent stated:

> I don't want to talk to anybody about my grandchildren being with me. I just tell people, when they ask me about my grandchildren being with me, that the children's parents and I have decided that the children should live with me for a while. I give no further discussion. It's too embarrassing.

Some of the grandparents in this study are attempting to heal their ruptured social life by creating a new social circle that focuses on solving their problems. One example of this is the GAP support group, which has been a positive social alternative for grandparents who share the common fate of feeling alienated from a more typical social life for grandparents.

The impact of stigma on the grandparents' emerging new social life is powerful. Social evasion and distancing occur because of the initial embarrassment over family circumstances. Cover-up of these circumstances can lead to emotional distress and dysfunction—to shame and fear, and to feeling judged and isolated. One's sense of self can be distorted by a perceived loss of reputation or, as Goffman (1963) called

Results

it, "spoiled identity." Goffman believed that this has the effect of cutting individuals off from their society and from themselves, so that they stand as discredited persons facing an unaccepting world. This sense of being social outcasts obviously has serious consequences for the well-being and happiness of the grandparents and their grandchildren.

One grandmother reported that parenting her grandchild and attempting to save her daughter from drug addiction have resulted in her loss of reputation and resources. Ms. E. reported, "I feel isolated from people in my age group. I feel I have no contact with my adult world. Here I am in surroundings that I've never ever lived in before, and I'm grateful that it's off the streets. It takes a lot of humility for me to sit here and tell you that I'm grateful for this." This grandmother felt that moving into a substandard neighborhood reflected her declining reputation, her increased stigma, and her eroded sense of self.

With the embarrassment and guilt of admitting her problems to her friends and social group, one grandmother felt like a "bubbling pot." "You can't separate anything," she said. "The vegetables are all there. I just try to deal with my feelings by attempting to sort things out." This grandmother felt especially guilty about betraying her family loyalty because she had exposed the family secret of her daughter's drug addiction.

Goffman (1959) noted that there is information about families that they knowingly conceal because it is incompatible with the self-image that they attempt to maintain and project to outsiders. Goffman believed that not all information in secrets is destructive. Secret-keeping, he argued, is a mechanism for protecting self-worth. Thus, many of the grandparents in this study have chosen to socially isolate themselves to avoid revealing compromising information about their adult children.

Black Grandparents As Parents

Loss of Leisure. Grandparents would like to have the choice of their leisure activities rather than the labor of parenting their grandchildren. They feel that they have approached the age and stage in their life where it is time for them to enjoy life and to pass on to others the duties of working and parenting (Cherlin & Furstenberg, 1986).

In the words of one grandmother, "I just want time to groom myself, to go take walks, to read and just do things for *me*. I would love to go visit my friends and relax. I feel so tired most of the time." Grandparents not only need "time out" for themselves; they have a social expectation that this is "owed" them.

The grandparents in this study feel "tied down" and robbed of their leisure options as they approach their retirement years. One grandparent reported:

> I've tried to sort out a lot of things that I have to do. Because of the responsibility of parenting my grandchildren, there are lots of demands on my time. Sometimes I feel closed in. Then I try to let go. There are times I just need a few minutes to rest. My grandchildren are always wanting my attention and time. I feel guilty at times when I can't deal with it because I need time for myself.

Another grandparent stated:

> Before I began parenting my grandchildren, I was involved in sewing, baking, political and community activities. I was doing things that I really enjoyed during my spare time. Now I have *no* spare time. I have no time where I can just sit and relax.

A grandparent who is parenting her three preschool grandchildren stated:

Results

> I seldom have time to do anything for myself. My day starts at 5:00 A.M. daily, in which I have to get my three grandchildren dressed, fed, and taken to babysitters and child-care before I have to catch my 7:00 A.M. train for work. Once I arrive at work, I feel so tired that I find myself falling to sleep.

This grandparent reports that she gets little sleep most nights because her two younger grandchildren were born "crack"-exposed. Thus, they are constantly ill and in need of medical attention. This requires the grandparent to spend many late-night hours holding, rocking, and attempting to console and comfort these grandbabies.

Loss of Independence. Control of their lives is a very important issue for these grandparents. They worked long and hard to get to a place where they could enjoy their independence. Now their entire lives are centered around parenting their grandchildren, and they have lost their prized independence. Ms. E. stated, "I don't have time to go shopping for myself and take care of some of my special personal needs. I need clothes and other necessities for myself. It is difficult for me to go shopping, including grocery shopping, because I have to dress all three grandbabies and take them with me." One grandparent indicated that it is difficult for her to find time even to go to the bathroom without someone knocking on the door and asking when she will be out.

In summary, as they approached their retirement years, the grandparents in this study looked forward to being involved in their grandchildren's lives, but not at the cost of their own autonomy, and not in the role of primary caretaker. They feel cheated out of socially prescribed expectations for this stage of their lives. They believe that they are making many personal and social sacrifices as they take on the parenting responsibility for their grandchildren. Since they have already raised their own children, they feel that they have "paid their dues" and now deserve the opportunity to enjoy their independent lives. The responsibility of parenting their grandchildren is causing them to feel "tied down" and robbed of their personhood, their independence. They feel deprived not only of their rights to be grandparents to their grandchildren but of having normal, healthy grandchildren as well.

Loss of Physical Health. The health of these grandparents suffers in this process. In general, they want to do more physically than they are actually capable of doing. As a result, they often sacrifice their own health needs. In addition, they create rationalizations for their poor health or illness that has been caused by their new burdens.

Many of these grandparents want to engage in more physical activity with their grandchildren, but are restrained by such age-related limitations as low energy, back problems, high blood pressure, and diabetes. Then they feel guilty and embarrassed that they don't have the capacity to provide more physical outlets for their grandchildren. Ms. E. stated:

> There are times I feel so guilty of not being able to do more physical things with my grandchildren that I find myself sacrificing my own feelings and health to accommodate them. I have one riding the bicycle while I'm trying to hold him up, one riding his tricycle, and I'm pushing one in the stroller, all at the same time.

Some grandparents ignore their own health issues as they focus on the medical, emotional, physical, and social needs of their grandchildren. They fear that their health is deteriorating; yet many don't have the energy or the money to do anything about it. They become frightened, helpless, and angry as they feel that all they once had is being taken away from them. One grandparent reported:

> I feel that I'm sacrificing all of my health needs to take care of my grandchildren. My whole life is a sacrifice for my grandchildren. I don't want them to feel like they are in poverty or that they are neglected. I want them to feel good about themselves. I just try to do what I can for them and pray that God will take care of me, so that I can be here for them.

For most of these grandparents, along with their medical problems comes a lack of patience and energy with the demands of their parenting responsibilities. One grandparent stated:

> I am sixty years old and have many medical problems of my own. I just can't keep up with the demands on my health and life. I can't sleep at night because I'm worrying about my grandchild and my own health. I need help because if something happens to me, I don't know who will take care of my grandchild. The fact that I can't sleep, and also the demands and expectations of me, cause me to feel tired and impatient.

The physical health of the grandparents can cause emotional stress and pressures on the grandchildren as well. Many of these children often worry about their grandparents' health. They fear that their grandparents may become ill and not be able to take care of them. One grandmother indicated that since she has been parenting her granddaughter for four years, the child has become very close to and dependent on her. "My granddaughter knows I have medical problems," she said, "and worries about me getting sick and leaving her. She said to me, 'Granny, if you die and leave me, I will kill myself, because I won't have anybody to take care of me.'"

Black Grandparents As Parents

Many of these grandparents wonder if their physical problems were caused by the stress they are experiencing as they parent their grandchildren. Interestingly, many of the grandparents do not view their physical problems as appropriate for this stage in their lives and seem to at least indirectly blame their adult children or their grandchildren for their infirmities. Stresses related to caring for the grandchildren may account for emotional upset or medical illnesses. One grandparent indicated that one of her grandchildren repeatedly disobeys her. He frequently runs away from home and often arrives home late from school. She describes this behavior as stressful and difficult for her, which keeps her emotionally upset. Ms. W., in her attempt to describe her physical pain and emotional stresses of parenting her grandchild, stated, "I feel so tired and stressed. I'm not sure if I'm medically ill, or if it's just stress and being overworked."

Some grandparents in this study felt that the ongoing emotional stresses of parenting their grandchildren have created severe medical problems for them. "I was rushed to the hospital last November," said Ms. D. "They thought I had a heart attack. It was just stress. I was in the hospital for a week. I was so worried about my grandchildren. My elderly mother took care of them for me. They were too much for her. I felt so guilty putting this responsibility on her." This grandparent clearly stated to me that she felt she was sacrificing her physical health to parent her three grandchildren.

Some grandparents in this study felt that the stress of learning that their adult children were addicted to drugs and the burdens of parenting of their grandchildren were simply too much for them to physically handle. "Because of the physical and emotional stress over the awareness of the drug addiction of my daughter and the parenting of my grandchildren," said Mr. D., "I felt suicidal. I just didn't know how to handle this stress." According to this grandparent, he spent thirty-eight days in the hospital with a heart attack, diabetes, high blood pressure, and other medical problems that nearly proved fatal.

Ms. A. reported:

> There are times I can't get up and down because of my back and legs hurting me. I guess I'm getting arthritis, because my back is beginning to cause me more problems. I can't do much walking now. It's a disadvantage to my grandchildren, because I'm just not physically able to do much with them.

In brief, many of the grandparents in this study believed that their deteriorating health was caused by the stress of raising their grandchildren and the pain of their adult children's drug involvement.

Financial Burdens. The financial issues around the parenting of their grandchildren have also been one of the primary concerns of the grandparents in this study. Most are experiencing "downward mobility" (from a position that was modest to begin with) and are increasingly dependent on others for financial support. Many are single women (divorced or widowed) who are on fixed incomes. However, a few of them have husbands who help out. As Ms. J. stated:

> My husband and I are in this together. He stands by me, and we do this together. There are many sacrifices that we have made and are still making as we continue to parent our four grandchildren. There are, of course, monetary sacrifices because, of course, even though we get Aid to Families with Dependent Children [AFDC], it costs an awful lot to raise children. We have to share some of our money with taking care of them and knowing that we will have to do more

because we want them to get in college. We have to prepare
for that.

Many of these grandparents initially receive no financial assistance
at all for their grandchildren, because the children were not placed with
them through the social-service system. A number of the grandparents
in this study rescued their grandchildren after they were abandoned by
their parents. Later, however, they sought financial assistance for their
grandchildren, once they became the primary parents for these children.

Some grandparents report that even though their grandchildren
receive AFDC, the check is frequently made out to the biological parent
with the child's name on it. In many cases, the biological parents then
use the checks to support their drug addiction. One grandparent in this
situation said of her daughter, "Oh, she might give me fifty dollars once
in a while for her child. She uses my grandchild's check to support her
drug habit. I can't get Social Service to see that."

Some grandparents in this study reported going to the Department
of Social Services or to Child Protective Services with proof that their
grandchildren were living with them, to no avail. Their hope was to have
the AFDC checks addressed to and made payable to them. "I even
invited the social worker to my house to show her my grandchildren's
clothes in the closet, their bedroom with their beds, their toys," said one
grandparent. Social Service agencies apparently disregard these realities by explaining that the biological parent is still the legal guardian of
these grandchildren. Grandparents spend many hours with these agencies in an attempt to get legal custody of their grandchildren. The
problem is that they are reluctant to bring criminal charges against their
own adult children. "I just don't know what else to do," one grandparent
stated. "My daughter comes around only for the grandchildren's checks,

and I seldom see her after that. She uses this money to support her drug habit." Those grandparents who do have physical custody or legal guardianship of their grandchildren, however, do receive AFDC or foster care payments for their grandchildren.

Social-service agencies also may contribute unwittingly to the poor health of the biological parents. One grandmother stated:

> I've gone to Social Service many times, trying to get financial help for my grandchild. My daughter continues to get the AFDC check for this child, even though she does not take care of him. It seems as if the Social Service is condoning my daughter's drug habit by continuing to give her the money.

Another grandmother reported:

> I had been on medical disability for two years before I began parenting my grandchildren. I was living alone and was making it. Once I began parenting my grandchildren, it was six months before I received any financial assistance for them. I used all the money I had saved. I couldn't pay my bills, my house note, or anything. I lost all my credit and could not get anything. This was difficult and embarrassing for me.

These policies also contribute to the impoverishment of these grandparents, many of whom receive less financial support for their grandchildren than do children who are placed in foster care with nonrelatives. One grandmother with two grandchildren in her care stated:

> The city expects us to take care of our grandchildren out of the goodness of our hearts. We take the burden off the Social Service system. They hardly give us anything in return. Most of us are barely able to make ends meet.

Black Grandparents As Parents

Another grandmother stated:

> There is a constant strain on my income since I began
> parenting my grandchildren. I'm constantly feeling ex-
> hausted from trying to work and raise my grandchildren. I
> only receive about three hundred dollars [AFDC] per month
> per child from the City Department of Social Services,
> compared with the nearly thousand dollars a month that is
> allotted for children who are in licensed group or foster
> homes.

Some grandparents who qualify for Social Security Disability Insurance (SSDI) because of a medical disability continue to work to support their grandchildren. One grandmother reported that because of the absence of adequate financial assistance for her grandchildren, she returned to work even though she had been placed on medical disability from her job before she began parenting her grandchildren.

Legal Guardianship. Grandparents in this study who opted for legal guardianship of their grandchildren felt that they needed to do penance for their perceived poor parenting of their own children. These grandparents also have concerns about having their grandchildren with them permanently. Most of these children were exposed to emotional traumas when they were with their biological parents. Approximately 53 percent of the grandparents in this study have either legal guardianship or formal custody of their grandchildren (see Appendix B). They indicated that, because of the drug addiction of their adult children, they felt responsible for the physical and emotional well-being of their grandchildren. They also felt angry at their children for exposing their grandchildren to these situations and for forcing this choice upon them.

Results

The grandchildren who were placed with their grandparents through legal channels were, in most cases, substance-exposed *in utero*, physically and/or sexually abused, abandoned, neglected, or rejected. In brief, these children had the most severely involved cases of child neglect. The involvement of Social Services in such cases has been increasing recently, making it easier for grandparents to opt for legal guardianship of their grandchildren. Grandparents seek permanent custody of their grandchildren to avoid threats of foster placement with nonrelatives. In these cases, the grandchildren themselves receive the support checks and are protected from exploitation by their biological parents.

However, approximately 47 percent of the grandparents in this study do not have either legal guardianship or formal custody of their grandchildren (see Appendix B). They hope that their own children will recover from their drug addiction and take the grandchildren back. In most cases, these are the offspring of teenage girls, some of whom may even continue to live in the grandparents' home but without contributing to the children's care. According to one grandparent, "All I want my daughter to do is get her life together so that she can get her children back. I will do whatever I can to support her in recovering from her drug addiction. She needs her children, and her children need her." These grandparents view the placement of their grandchildren with them as temporary.

Summary. The grandparents in this study experienced a wide variety of changes in their lives. Paramount among these was the disruption of their expectations as they entered their retirement years.

Black Grandparents As Parents

Their hoped-for realities were crushed by the impact of drug use on their own children's lives. Not only did they take on the new and difficult responsibility of rearing small and, in some instances, handicapped children, but they were also faced with the almost insurmountable task of rebuilding their own lives and restoring their sense of self.

4

Discussion

Emotional Impact

Never before in the recent history of Western societies has such a large number of grandparents been reported to be serving as surrogate parents to their grandchildren. Studies such as the present one are imperative if, as a society, we want to deal responsibly with the implications of these new developments in parenting for black families in particular, as well as for other families who face similar dilemmas.

Traditionally, grandparents have played significant roles in the lives of their grandchildren, often providing substantial help and stability to their children's children. Grandparents traditionally invest both time and commitment in establishing supportive and compassionate relationships with their grandchildren (Cherlin & Furstenberg, 1986). Accordingly, most contemporary grandparents are only marginally involved in rearing their grandchildren. In most of today's families, as Cherlin and Furstenberg note, grandparents serve as a latent source of support to their grandchildren, ready to step in when needed.

Black Grandparents As Parents

Contrary to this norm, the grandparents interviewed for the present study are performing the primary role of parenting their grandchildren. They are being deprived of enjoying traditional grandparent-grandchild relationships as well as a loving relationship with their own adult children.

While studying how these grandparents have taken on the responsibility of parenting their grandchildren, I found virtually no research on the emotional impact of this kind of arrangement on (1) the children, (2) the grandparents, or (3) the children's biological parents. As a clinician who works with such grandparents, I have seen the profound impact that this arrangement can have on all family members. My research shows that the emotional impact is mainly shaped by a process involving (1) the grandparents' awareness of the drug involvement of their adult children, (2) revised family systems, (3) altered self-concepts, particularly among the grandparents and grandchildren, and (4) the grandparents' developmental incongruities.

Awareness of the Adult Children's Drug Use. In spite of the love that these grandparents have for their adult children, they have a difficult time reconciling this love with their children's drug addiction. These ambivalent feelings prevent them from letting go of their children to the drug world. In the process, they often long to create in the present and reconstruct from the past an idealized family life.

The rupture in their family ties created by the drug addiction of their adult children leads to anxiety and frustration. This also has a negative impact on the relationship between the grandparents and the grandchil-

Discussion

dren. These dysfunctional characteristics of their family are not congruent with their idea of normalcy. Some tend to contrast their present life with an imaginary idealized past. They may create unrealistic expectations for their grandchildren in an unconscious recapitulation of their expectations for their own children.

The "bed of roses" fantasies that some of the grandparents create about their younger years are not supported by the evidence, since most of these grandparents were in fact single parents who had many problems raising their children. Their current fantasies not only are a disservice to their relationship with their own children but also deny them and their children the tools needed to cope with their present-day problems. Sacrifice seems to be the pivotal experience that "justifies" and fuels the fantasy. Because the grandparents made sacrifices for their children, they believed and expected that life owed them a better outcome. Now that their sacrifices for their children have "betrayed" them, they are trying to re-create a "normal" family life that never truly existed in the past.

In the present study, there were two distinct patterns for expressing this orientation toward future life satisfaction. I found that those grandparents who had no prior warning that their children would choose to become involved with drugs were more likely to emphasize their feelings of *betrayal*. These grandparents were more likely to express the desire to—and to actually—return their grandchildren to the biological parents.* They were also more likely to want to reconnect with their own

---

*Of the fourteen grandparents whom I interviewed for this study, four were in this betrayal category. Two of them ultimately returned their grandchildren to the biological parents.

relinquished lives and reestablish concepts of former selves. These were the grandparents with the strongest feelings of *deprivation*. They were most highly motivated to restore the normal parent-child and grandparent-grandchild relationship and to reclaim their past goals and lifestyles.

In contrast, those grandparents who were more apt to feel *guilty* about possible inadequacies in their own child-rearing practices were those who said they experienced a creeping awareness that their adult children were engaging in troublesome behavior. These grandparents were more likely to seek legal guardianship of their grandchildren and were more apt to strive to succeed at reparenting, because they felt the need to do a better job of parenting the second time. One important aspect of this difference between grandparents is that those who got a rude shock regarding the drug behavior of their children were better able to disconnect from the drug problems and let their children take responsibility. The other grandparents were still caught up in long-standing denial about the problems, as though they themselves were co-addicts.

Revised Family Systems. Individual families in both groups find different solutions to their particular family challenges. The main consequence is a weakened authority structure in the home. As grandchildren attempt to deal with their ambivalent feelings toward being parented by their grandparents, they seem anxious and confused about the absence of their biological parents in their life. Anxiety is seen by Bowlby (1960) as a primary response to the rupture of attachment to the mother. Failures in "good-enough" mothering, Winnicott (1960) notes, lead to distortions of the ego and the developments of a false self and ego splitting in the child.

Discussion

In some instances, there is a multigenerational family structure in which the grandparents, the parents, and the grandchildren all live together in the grandparents' home. Three of the fourteen grandparents in the present study continue to have their adult children living in their home (see Appendix C). This multigenerational arrangement, however, can create a blurred family structure that confuses the grandchildren because they are unable to bond exclusively with their biological parents. They develop divided loyalties between their biological parents and their grandparents, and thus they often feel torn between the parental figures in the home. Needless to say, this creates additional stress for the grandparents.

Another variation in family arrangements occurs when the biological parents live in the same community rather than the same home as the grandparents, but continue to visit their children. While the authority lines are somewhat clearer in this case, the biological parents compete for and undermine the parental authority of the grandparents when they are alone with the children. These grandchildren receive yet another variety of confusing parental messages that are divided and diluted.

In addition, a large number of these biological parents live on the streets and are frequently incarcerated because of their drug addiction and illicit behaviors. The grandparents worry about their physical and emotional safety and feel guilty about not providing them with a home. This diverts attention away from the grandchildren at a time when their need for care is great.

In contrast, when their adult children are incarcerated, grandparents feel relieved by knowing where they are. Several grandparents whose sons or daughters have been incarcerated reported to me that at least they were able to sleep and not worry about their children's physical safety.

But some grandparents feel responsible for the incarceration of their adult children despite the safety it provides them, and they search for ways to have them released. Grandchildren feel angry and confused because they condemn their parents' condition but still want to feel good about them. They look to themselves or others to blame for their dilemma. Some grandparents will take the older grandchildren to see their incarcerated parents. This helps the children to accept their painful realities. Although the parenting focus of the grandparents is stronger and better defined in this case, the relationships between the grandparents and their adult children are exacerbated by the latter's incarceration.

Once they have been released from incarceration, the adult children frequently return to live with their parents. Grandparents feel a sense of commitment to take their children back into the home, hoping that their incarceration has forced a change in their commitment to recover from their substance abuse. This takes the family back into a multigenerational structure, which may revive the confusion around parenting boundaries for the grandchildren and precipitate another cycle of family disruptions.

Finally, some biological parents frequently disappear and may not see their children for long periods of time. The children worry about their parents, wondering if they are alive and where they are. The grandparents also worry about the safety and whereabouts of their adult children and feel abandoned by them. In these circumstances, the grandparents ostensibly have total authority over their grandchildren. But the disappearance of the parents profoundly affects the relationship and bonding between the grandparents and grandchildren, with the

Discussion

parent often becoming an unseen competing authority figure that is quite intrusive in the parenting structure of the grandchildren. One consequence, when the symbolic figurehead is missing, is to heap blame on someone who is present. Grandchildren may hold the grandparents responsible for the disappearance of their parents, or they may assume the blame themselves. Grandparents, in turn, may blame the grandchildren or become consumed with self-blame.

In spite of the abuse that some of these children have experienced from their biological parents, many continue to love them and feel a strong sense of loyalty to them. Although they may feel angry toward their parents for abandoning them, they are also concerned that loving their grandparents may mean that they are abandoning their parents. Some children run away from their grandparents' home in search of their parents. Others inflict self-punishment as an escape—up to and attempting suicide.

The concerns of these grandparents reflect Colon's (1978) view that a child's experience of biological familial continuity is of prime importance in establishing a sense of self and personal significance. Colon made a strong case for children's need to have access to their biological "rootedness," observing that a child who has ruptures in the "attachment" process of familial bonding will have trouble trusting and opening up to other persons. Colon further notes that children who have been cut off from their parents are likely to duplicate destructive family patterns in their interpersonal and family relationships.

Self-Image/Stigmas. Self-image is negatively affected in all these developments. Many grandparents feel socially isolated and excluded from their peer group. In particular, the drug addiction of their adult children is too embarrassing and painful for them to disclose to their relatives and friends—most of whom see through their "front" anyway.

The more affluent grandparents feel more isolated from their peer group and social circles because of their fear of negative labels. They have a powerful investment in their family image and fear that their whole family will be judged negatively because of the drug addiction of their children, thereby undermining the influence that they perceive comes with their status. Thus, they feel uncomfortable admitting to their friends and peers the true reasons they are parenting their grandchildren. They know they aren't fooling their friends, and they feel ashamed about the exposure of their family life. The less affluent grandparents, however, do not feel the same degree of social risk even though they experience the same self-isolation. Indictment for breaches of norms in higher status groups is apparently more severe.

The grandparents in this study feel that they have acquired a negative identity from their grandchildren—that their parenting responsibilities have turned them from loving grandparents into "mean old ladies." Goffman (1963) reported that there are some stigmas that are so easily concealed that they figure very little in the individual's relationships with acquaintances. A negative stigma, Goffman noted, and the effort to conceal or remedy it, may become "fixed" as part of a person's identity. Negative stigmas of this type have interfered with the warm and positive relationships that these grandparents expected with their grandchildren. They long for the role of grandparent, not parent, to the children.

Discussion

Developmental Dissonance. The grandparents in this study feel robbed of socially prescribed expectations for this stage of their life. Neugarten (1968) noted that events that occur at the socially or developmentally appropriate time are rarely a crisis in our lives. However, life events that occur too early or too late in life are the most traumatic. The traumatic experience for these grandparents was giving up their role as traditional grandparents. They have given up their privacy. They have given up control over their lives and their independence. They have lost their leisure. They feel tied down and robbed of their personhood. They are not living the conventional life stages that they have always known and looked forward to.

Kivnik (1982) reported that grandparenthood is more significant for those who have experienced social losses, giving relationships with grandchildren compensatory functions. Grandparents in the present study have experienced a variety of social losses. Many have lost one or more children to drug addiction—and with that, they have often lost their identity as good parents. They also have lost their identity as grandparents and the commensurate comfort it ostensibly brings. In the process, they switch from the role of being grandparents to being parents to their grandchildren. Kegan (1982) noted that "the shift from one role to the next can be painful, protracted, and life disordering" (p. 207). The threat of the loss of this important grandparent-grandchild relationship is potentially the precipitating experience for crisis. This is another impediment to forming an ideal family.

In discussing changes that occur in all individuals as they age, Neugarten (1968) suggested that we look to the social as well as the biological clock and to social definitions of age and age-appropriate behaviors and expectations. Levinson (1978), in his study of the adult life course, noted that the life structure is the pattern or design of a person's life, a meshing of self in world. This is a primary component, he argued, in one's relationship with self, other persons, groups, and institutions, and with all aspects of the external world that have significance to one's life.

Contrary to these popular theoretical ideas about life development, the grandparents in the present study have regressed to stages in their past lives rather than moved on to new ones. This has created dissonance for them. This dissonance has partly been created out of the experience of losing their future goals. The grandparents have adjusted to this strain in a variety of ways. Some have reconnected with threads of former goals and a sense of a former self. Others have put their lives on hold. In extreme cases, grandparents have totally relinquished their wished-for lives and their sense of self. Nevertheless, their new experience still feels incongruous to them.

Physical and Economic Adjustments

While the emotional impact is most salient for therapists, the practical consequences of the changes in the lives of grandparents and grandchildren cannot be ignored. The two are interdependent. Structural changes have critically influenced the emotional life of these grandparents. For many of them, these changes have included physical adjustments, deteriorating health, and downward economic mobility.

Discussion

One of the most important adjustments that these grandparents had to make was to move their residence to accommodate their grandchildren. In some cases, the grandparents had moved to smaller, one-bedroom living spaces after their own children had grown up and moved away. This initial uprooting from the family home was already very stressful. Brown and Harris (1978) noted that, while moving is stressful at any age, it is particularly stressful for older people because of the importance of neighborhood-based social relations. Arling (1976) stated that for the older, retired population, their neighborhood or immediate residential environment is often their best source of friendship. As a result, their neighborhood is likely to contain many important, long-term relationships.

The grandparents in this study expressed feeling chronically displaced as they relocated with their grandchildren from their adopted adult residential environment into yet another environment. Grandparents living in one-bedroom apartments suddenly found themselves sharing their bed with one or more grandchildren. Thus, they had to seek larger, more appropriate living spaces. They also were faced with the need to collect appropriate furniture for their grandchildren. In addition, they had to relearn the rules of housekeeping with small children. This produced significant stress, anxiety, and financial strain for the grandparents.

The grandparents in this study also had to readjust their daily schedules and deal with revised work schedules due to their grandchildren's daily needs. Child-care was the central scheduling problem. The serious health problems of many of these grandchildren required frequent readjustments in child-care arrangements. The grandparents were often called from their jobs to attend medical or school emergencies for their grandchildren. This caused them to become less dependable employees, and some of them lost their jobs because of this intrusion in their work schedules and job performances.

Most of the grandparents in this study revised their social agendas. Travel had been important to all of them because they saw this as their social outlet during their retirement years. The more affluent ones had more extensive travel plans to relinquish. But all of them created new social agendas for themselves through support groups, churches, child-care agencies, and schools, among other community resources. Their grandchildren's school life became an integral part of their social schedule.

Health Issues. The grandparents in this study longed to engage in more physical activities with their grandchildren, but along with age often come physical limitations such as low energy, back problems, high blood pressure, and diabetes. Grandparents often ignore their health issues and needs as they focus on the health care of their grandchildren. They fear that their health is deteriorating, yet many of them don't have the energy or money to take care of themselves.

Some grandparents wonder if their health problems are the result of the emotional stress of parenting their grandchildren as they feel robbed of their own adult life. There is a tendency here for them to blame their grandchildren for their own physical ailments. They also blame their adult children, because the stresses of learning that their sons or daughters were addicted to drugs and that they would have to take over the parenting of their grandchildren were too much for them to handle physically. The grandparents in this study felt frightened and worried

Discussion

over the possibility that their grandchildren might adopt the same malignant lifestyle and environment as their biological parents. Some of the grandparents view illness and death as an escape for themselves.

All the grandchildren in this study have varying degrees of emotional and physical health problems related to their abandonment by their parents. They have experienced physical and/or sexual abuse, abandonment, and rejection by their parents. Those who were prenatal "crack"-exposed infants needed constant medical attention and cost grandparents many sleepless nights. As a result of prenatal "crack" exposure, a number of these grandbabies had low birthweight and were developmentally delayed. Many are still experiencing visual and auditory impairments. Some have severe speech impediments and emotional problems. Many have frequent medical emergencies, causing them to be hospitalized for varying periods. Several of them are hyperactive. The grandparents have a difficult time containing or managing the behavior of these children.

The older grandchildren were born before the "crack" epidemic. Nevertheless, some of these youths also experienced physical and/or sexual abuse or abandonment by their parents and have serious emotional and social problems in school and the community. Under these devastating conditions, the idealized family that the grandparents anticipated turned into a nightmare.

Economics/Downward Mobility. Many grandparents in the present study feel that the financial responsibilities of parenting their grandchildren continue to be one of their primary burdens. A number of them are experiencing "downward financial mobility" with an increasing dependence on others (often family members) for financial support. At the time that they assumed the parenting responsibility of their grandchildren, some of them had retired primarily because of medical disability or age, and now were driven back into the work force. Others, who had not retired, now lost their jobs because of this disruption in their lives.

Although some of the grandparents are helped by Aid for Families with Dependent Children (AFDC), Medical Disability, Social Security Disability Insurance (SSDI), and/or subsidized housing, they often use their own savings to supplement the small amount of public assistance they receive for their grandchildren. The need to revise Child Welfare policies based on this evidence seems obvious and urgent.

Limitations of the Study

Although this study has unveiled significant issues and exposed the needs and experiences of grandparents who are parenting their grandchildren, the most obvious limitation of the research is its restriction to grandparents who could find their way to a support group. This was a very specialized group. Because these grandparents sought help and searched for available resources, they probably have greater psychological and social resources available to them and experience less social isolation than grandparents who do not or cannot seek such help.

Two other significant limitations of the research are the small size of the sample population and its geographical restriction to the Oakland area of northern California. Although common themes emerged from the grandparents in one-on-one interviews and in the Grandparents As Parents support group, additional data might be revealed using a larger, more geographically diversified study population.

Discussion

Another limitation of this study is the difficulty I had in finding relevant literature and other resources specifically related to the subject of grandparents who are the primary caretakers of their grandchildren. The literature in this area is extremely limited, so I hope this study will begin to fill the void.

Directions for Future Research

This study has focused on grandparents who are surrogate parents to their grandchildren primarily because of the drug epidemic and/or the incarceration of the biological parents. Future research should focus on grandparents who are parenting their grandchildren because of the death or divorce of the biological parents. Comparing grandparents in the two different types of situation may yield similar yet different experiences and themes.

Future research in this area should also identify additional community and social resources that may be used by grandparents as they parent their grandchildren. The profiles in this study of grandparents as parents may have exposed not only social and psychological issues but the need for additional social and political action to address the needs of these grandparents.

Another promising area of investigation would be to explore the differences between grandmothers and grandfathers as surrogate parents to their grandchildren—a topic only briefly alluded to here because of lack of available subjects. Many grandchildren who are parented by their grandmothers have *no* male role models in their families.

Black Grandparents As Parents

A related subject that could be explored in depth is the variety of problems that arise when grandparents have some adult children who responsibly parent their own offspring and other adult children who do not. Rivalry often develops between grandchildren who get to experience their grandparents more or less as Santa Claus and their cousins who experience their grandparents as parental disciplinarians.

Additional inquiries that will of necessity have to be made in the future are longitudinal studies of the three generations examined here: the grandparents, their adult children, and their grandchildren. Questions might include: What happens to the grandparents in the long term? How many of the adult children ultimately kick their drug habit and lead productive lives, including taking back the responsibility of parenting their children? What kinds of lives do the grandchildren ultimately lead? How many are mentally or physically disabled because of their parents' drug abuse? How many repeat their grandparents' worst fears by themselves becoming drug addicts? And, in the *very* long term, what happens to the children of the grandchildren, who will probably never know what it is like to have grandparents at all?

Implications for Policy and Treatment

While the role of grandparents as parents has become an increasingly common phenomenon in today's society, there has been an absence of political sensitivity and a lack of recognition even of the needs of this population. It is my fervent hope that this study will increase social and political awareness among the general public and particularly among social-service agencies and policy-making bodies,

94

Discussion

so that they become more understanding of the problems and more involved in finding solutions. I especially hope that policymakers will pass and implement major legislation that will allow for meaningful financial and legal resources and assistance for this population of grandparents.

In this respect, California Assemblyman Tom Bates (1989, 1990) has been very helpful. As the chairman of the Committee on Human Services, he has held frequent hearings on issues related to the present subject and has introduced legislation that focuses on financial support for special needs children, particularly those who have physical, mental, or emotional handicaps as a result of their exposure to drugs or alcohol *in utero*. Unfortunately, his bill has twice been vetoed by the governor.

There is also a need for realistic health-care policies, both for physical and mental health, that will focus on the grandparents' own health needs, as well as those of their drug-addicted children and their drug-affected grandchildren. There are clinical implications in my findings as well. Most of the grandparents I interviewed experienced emotional upheavals as they became parents to their grandchildren; yet many of them ignored or denied their emotional turmoil. Their anger, embarrassment, and guilt are sensitive areas for them because of family loyalty and their reluctance to expose family secrets. In some cases, these grandparents were not even aware that therapeutic resources exist to help them. Hopefully, this study will assist other grandparents to acknowledge the emotional impact that their new role has on their lives and to be aware of the therapeutic options available to them. Services such as the Grandparents As Parents support groups can provide important social outlets and peer acceptance for these grandparents. GAP groups can also establish auxiliary support groups for the grandchildren. Perhaps divided into three age categories (say, 6–10, 11–13, and 14–17), such groups could supplement the one-on-one therapy that some of the children already get and put them in contact with peers who have similar feelings and experiences.

There is also clearly a need for an umbrella organization to serve as a privately funded autonomous advocacy group for grandparents who take over the parenting responsibility of their grandchildren. Such a group could operate an 800-number informational switchboard, sponsor research and lectures, push for legislative programs, call press conferences to draw attention to urgent problems, and run ads in the media to raise public consciousness about various issues.

Finally, it would be extremely helpful if there were a national charitable foundation devoted to raising funds that could be dispersed both to organizations involved with this cause and to worthy individual grandparents themselves as they struggle to be parents a second time around.

References

Accinelli, L. (1988, September 11). Starting over. *Daily Breeze* (Los Angeles), p. 20.

Apple, D. (1956). The social structure of grandparenthood. *American Anthropologist, 58,* 656–663.

Arling, G. (1976). The elderly widow and her family, neighbors, and friends. *Journal of Marriage and the Family, 38,* 757–868.

Atchley, R. C., Miller, S. J., & Troll, L. E. (1979). *Families in later life.* Belmont, CA: Wadsworth.

Benedek, T. (1959). Parenthood as a developmental phase. *Journal of the American Psychoanalytic Association, 7,* 389–417.

Bengston, V. L., & Robertson, J. F. (1985). *Grandparenthood.* Beverly Hills, CA: Sage.

Blumenfeld, E. S. (1983, December). *The study of a woman's college class thirty years later: Maturity in middle–aged women.* Doctoral dissertation, Institute for Clinical Social Work, Berkeley, CA.

Blumer, H. (1969). *Symbolic interactionalism: Perspective and method.* Englewood Cliffs, NJ: Prentice-Hall.

Boarder babies linger in hospitals. (1989, September 11). *Washington Post,* pp. A13, A14.

Bongaarts, J., Menken, J. A., & Watkins, S. C. (1984, October). Continuities and changes in the American family. Paper presented at the annual meeting of the Social Science History Association, Toronto, Canada.

Black Grandparents As Parents

Bowlby, J. (1960). Separation anxiety. *International Journal of Psychoanalysis, 41*, 89–113.

Brooks, D. (1989, September 10). These kids deserve life. *The Sunday Argus* (Hayward, CA), pp. 37–38.

Brown, G. I., & Harris, T. (1978). *Social origins of depression.* New York: Macmillan.

Charmaz, K. (1990). "Discovering" chronic illness: Using grounded theory. Paper presented at Sonoma State University, Rohnert Park, CA.

Cherlin, A. J., & Furstenberg, F., Jr. (1986). *The new American grandparent: A place in the family, a life apart.* New York: Basic Books.

Colon, F. (1978). Family ties and the child placement. *Family Process, 17*, 289–312.

DeToledo, S. (1988, October). Personal communication. Psychiatric Clinic for Youth, Long Beach, CA.

Farrar, H. C., & Kearns, G. (1989, November). Cocaine: Clinical pharmacology and toxicology. *The Journal of Pediatrics, 115*(5), 667–670.

Franklin, N. B. (1989). *Black families in therapy.* New York: Guilford.

Freud, S. (1963). *Therapy and techniques.* New York: Macmillan.

Freud, S. (1965). *New introductory lectures in psychoanalysis* (J. Strachey, Ed. & Trans.). New York: W. W. Norton.

Furstenberg, F., Jr. (1980). Reflections of remarriage. *Journal of Family Issues, 1*, 443–454.

Glaser, B. G. (1978). *Advances in the methodology of grounded theory: Theoretical sensitivity.* Mill Valley, CA: Sociology Press.

References

Glaser, B. G., & Strauss, A. L. (1969). *The discovery of grounded theory: Strategies for qualitative research*. San Francisco: University of California Medical Center.

Glick, P. C. (1985). Demographic picture of Black families. In H. P. McAdoo (Ed.), *Black families*. Beverly Hills, CA: Sage.

Goffman, E. (1959). *The presentation of self in everyday life*. New York: Anchor.

Goffman, E. (1963). *Stigma: Notes on the management of spoiled identity*. Englewood Cliffs, NJ: Prentice-Hall.

Grandmothers on the line. (1989, November 17). *East Bay Express* (Berkeley, CA), pp. 3, 28.

Grandmothers struggle to pick up where parents left off. (1989, September 10). *Washington Post*, pp. A23, A24.

Grau, L., & Susser, I. (1989). *Women in later years: Health, social, and cultural perspectives*. New York: Harrington Park Press.

Hagestad, G. O. (1985). Continuity and connectedness. In V. Bengston & J. Robertson (Eds.), *Grandparenthood*. Beverly Hills, CA: Sage.

Hancock, E. (1981). *Women's development in adult life*. Doctoral dissertation, Harvard University, Cambridge, MA.

Henig, R. M. (1988). *The myth of senility*. Rev. ed. Glenview, IL: Scott, Foresman.

Jackson, J. (1980). *Minorities and aging*. Belmont, CA: Wadsworth.

Johnson, C. L. (1983). A cultural analysis of the grandmother. *Social Gerontology and Adult Development*, *5*(4), whole issue.

Johnson, C. L. (1985). Grandparenting options in divorcing families. In V. Bengston & J. Robertson (Eds.), *Grandparenthood*. Beverly Hills, CA: Sage.

Johnson, C. L. (1987). *Marital instability and the changing kinship networks of grandparents*. San Francisco: Gerontological Society of America.

Johnson, C. L. (1988). *Active and latent function of grandparenting during the divorce process*. San Francisco: Gerontological Society of America.

Jones, F. C. (1973). The lofty role of the black grandmother. *Crisis, 80*, 19–21.

Jung, C. G. (1971). The stages of life. In J. Campbell (Ed.), *The portable Jung*. New York: Viking.

Kegan, R. (1982). *The evolving self: Problems and process in human development*. Cambridge, MA: Harvard University Press.

Kivnik, H. (1982). Grandparenthood: An overview of meaning and mental health. *Gerontologist, 22*, 59–66.

LaMotte, R. (1988, March). Personal communication. Los Angeles County Department of Children's Services, Los Angeles, CA.

Lawson, D. (1988, May 22). Becoming a parent again. *Los Angeles Times*, p. 8.

Levinson, D. (1978). *The seasons of a man's life*. New York: Knopf.

Lewis, K. D., Bennett, B., & Schmeder, N. H. (1989, September/October). The care of infants menaced by cocaine abuse. *MCN, 14*, 324–328.

McAdoo, H. P. (1985). *Black families*. Beverly Hills, CA: Sage.

McCall, G., & Simmons, J. L. (1969). *Issues in participant observation*. Reading, MA: Addison-Wesley.

Mauluccio, A., & Sinonoglu, P. (1981). *Working with parents of children in foster care*. New York: Child Welfare of America.

References

Miller, J. B. (1976). *Toward a new psychology of women.* Boston: Beacon.

Nagy, J., & Spark, G. (1973). *Invisible loyalties.* Hagertown, MD: Harper & Row.

Neugarten, B. (1968). Adult personality: Toward a psychology of the life cycle—Middle age and aging. Paper presented to a social psychology conference at the University of Chicago.

Newberg, C. (1989, May 25). Heroic grandmothers raising many "crack" kids. *Oakland Tribune,* pp. 10, 12.

O'Connell, M. [Chief of the Fertility Statistics Branch of the United States Bureau of the Census]. (1988, May 22). Becoming a parent again. *Los Angeles Times,* pp. 7, 8.

Roscow, I. (1976). Status and role changes through the life span. In R. E. Binstock & E. Shanas (Eds.), *Handbook of aging and the social sciences.* New York: Van Nostrand Reinhold.

Saltz, R. (1970). *Effects of a foster grandparent program on the intellectual and social development of young children in an institution.* Doctoral dissertation, Wayne State University, Detroit, MI.

Schatzman, L., & Strauss, A. L. (1973). *Field research.* Inglewood Cliffs, NJ: Prentice-Hall.

Schneider, D. (1968). *American kinship: A cultural account.* Englewood Cliffs, NJ: Prentice-Hall.

Sprey, J., & Matthews, S. (1981). The impact of divorce on grandparenting. Paper presented at the Gerontological Society of America, Toronto, Canada.

Staples, R. (1971). *The Black family: Essays and studies.* Belmont, CA: Wadsworth.

Stone, D. [Reporter for the Pacific News Service]. (1989, November). Personal communication.

Strauss, A. L. (1987). *Qualitative analysis for social scientists.* Cambridge, England: Cambridge University Press.

Strauss, A. L., & Corbin, J. (1990). *Basics of qualitative research.* Beverly Hills, CA: Sage.

Sullivan, Harry S. (1954). *The psychiatric interview.* New York: W. W. Norton.

Sweeney, W. [Alameda County presiding juvenile judge]. (1989, September). *Viewpoints* (Oakland, CA), p. 1.

The 21st century family: Special edition. (1990, Winter/Spring). *Newsweek.*

Winnicott, D. (1960). The theory of the parent-infant relationship. *International Journal of Psycho-Analysis, 41,* 585–595.

Appendix A

Rate of "Crack"-Cocaine Exposure of Grandchildren

Code	Number of children	Number exposed to "crack"	Ages of children exposed	Number not exposed to "crack"
001	2	2	2, 3 years	0
002	1	0	—	1
003	1	1	3 years	0
004	1	1	3 years	0
005	3	1	6 years	2
006	2	1	6 years	1
007	2	0	—	2
008	1	0	—	1
009	3	1	9 years	2
010	2	0	—	2
011	4	2	2 years	2
012	1	0	—	1
013	3	2	12 months	1
014	4	1	12 months	3
	$n = 30$	12 = 40%		18 = 60%

Appendix B

Legal Guardianship/Formal Custody

Code	Legal Guardianship	Informal Custody
001	0	2
002	1	0
003	1	0
004	0	1
005	3	0
006	0	2
007	2	0
008	0	1
009	3	0
010	0	2
011	2	2
012	0	1
013	3	0
014	1	3
($n = 30$)	16 = 53%	14 = 47%

Appendix C

Biological Parents Living in the Home

Code	Number
001	0
002	0
003	0
004	1
005	0
006	0
007	0
008	0
009	0
010	0
011	0
012	1
013	1
014	0
($n = 14$)	$3 = 21\%$

Appendix D

Contacts with Public and Child-Serving Agencies

Al-Mateen, Majeed, M.D.
Pediatric Neurology
Children's Hospital Medical Center of Northern California
Oakland, California

Armstrong, Katherine
Richmond Mental Health
Richmond, California

Beckwinkel, Marie
Legal Aid Foundation
Los Angeles, California

Claxton, Sharon
Napa County Mental Health Association
Napa, California

Coon, Virginia
Dandiego, Sue
Foster Parent Association
New Jersey

DeToledo, Sylvia
Grandparents As Parents support group
Long Beach, California

Fields, Clavin
The National Center on Black Aged
The Institute of Gerontology
Washington, D.C.

Fink, Janet
Firestein, Rose
Children Placed with Relatives
New York

Holiday, Sandra
Chief of Medical Services
Highland General Hospital
Oakland, California

Jackson, James
Clinical Psychologist
School of Social Psychology
University of Michigan
Ann Arbor, Michigan

Johnson, Coleen
University of California at San Francisco
San Francisco, California

Johnson, Debra
School of Psychology
Berkeley, California

Labrie, Vida
University of California at San Francisco
San Francisco, California

LaMotte, Ray
Los Angeles County Department of Children's Services
Los Angeles, California

LePak, Dennis
Contra Costa County Probation Department
Concord, California

Lynch, Kim
Bananas, Inc.
Oakland, California

McAdoo, Harriet
McAdoo, John
Publishers, *The Black Families*
Washington, D.C.

Mumns, Joyce
Child Welfare League of America
Washington, D.C.

Pastermak, Sandy
Alameda County Health Care Service Agency
Oakland, California

Riegel, Betsey
The National Foster Placement Association
New Jersey

Shust, Diane
The House Select Committee on Children, Youth, and Families
Washington, D.C.

Snowden, Lonnie
Clinical Psychologist
School of Social Welfare
University of California
Berkeley, California

Solomon, Patty
Clinical Psychologist
The Vulnerable Child Care Center
Children's Hospital of the East Bay
Oakland, California

Stone, Deanne
Reporter
Pacific News Service
Berkeley, California